# Coping With Supervisory Nightmares

# Coping With Supervisory Nightmares

*12 Common Nightmares of Leadership and What You Can Do About Them*

**Michael and Deborah Singer Dobson**

**SkillPath® Publications**
**Mission, Kansas**

Editor: Jane Doyle Guthrie

Cover Design: Jason Sprenger

Library of Congress Catalog Card Number: 96-68883

ISBN: 1-57294-067-0

Printed in the United States of America

*This book is dedicated, with love, to our son,*

*James Alexander Singer Dobson*

# Contents

# How to Use This Book

*Coping With Supervisory Nightmares* is designed to meet two goals: to help the new supervisor identify potential dangers and head them off, and to help the supervisor suffering from a nightmare to develop a plan to solve it.

First, read or review Section 1 to understand the basic five-point strategy and the general process. Then, read the chapters that relate to your specific nightmares. If you don't find your particular nightmare in the book, the last chapter is a "do-it-yourself" exercise for creating a plan of attack.

The nightmares are divided into three sections:

- Employee Nightmares (your staff)

- Management Nightmares (your managers)

- Worklife Nightmares (everything else)

Each section begins with a detailed overview of the problems in that category, and then presents individual chapters ("Help!") covering the most common nightmares. You'll discover strategies for the most common problems as well as models you can adapt for other situations.

Because (hopefully!) you don't have *all* the nightmares described here, you don't necessarily need to read every single chapter, and you certainly don't have to read them in the order presented. However, some problems ("Help! I'm Supervising a Friend) are so common that it's probably a good idea to read the chapter even if it's not part of your current situation. The best time to solve a problem is *before* it turns into a nightmare.

# The Scope of Supervisory Nightmares

# What Is a Supervisory Nightmare?

Mama didn't tell you there'd be days like this.

You're supposed to be a supervisor, a person who provides guidance and direction, who serves as an interface between senior management and staff. You have your own work to do, your own problems, and suddenly the weight of the world comes crashing in.

The stress is getting to you. In the middle of the night, in the middle of a shower, in the middle of a pleasant dinner, your job comes rushing back into the center of your life. You start to obsess about the latest disaster, the nightmares that consume you—wide awake.

## Employee Nightmares

You thought Employee #1 was your friend; at least she was before you became a supervisor. Some friend. She doesn't do the work yet expects you not to take action because of your relationship, and she whines every time you give her an assignment not to her liking.

Then there's Employee #2. He wanted the supervisor's job and didn't get it. He had the necessary technical skills, and it's undeniable that he's competent. Why didn't he get the job? Lack of people skills. He's abrasive in his general manner and has antagonized most of his co-workers. Unfortunately, you can't make him understand that. It's all other people's fault. Employee #2 is convinced you got the job because of favoritism or discrimination, and he blames you. The best thing that could happen for him is for you to fail, because that would validate his claim of being treated unfairly.

Employee #3 has been with the company for a long time, and she knows everything. Absolutely everything. You can tell her what you want her to do, but she goes off and does what she "knows" to be right. "We've always done it that way," she says. "When you've been here as long as I have, you'll understand these things."

Employee #4 has such a commitment to quality that he regularly goes to your boss with detailed reports about failures and mistakes and problems in the department—all in the spirit of helpfulness, of course. He's often wrong in his observations, but he does get listened to, and your credibility crumbles.

## Management Nightmares

In the realm of supervisory nightmares, let's not forget your own supervisors, who can undercut your position even more effectively than those you oversee.

Maybe your supervisor is into conflict avoidance. Just try to face any issues directly with this fellow and watch him run for cover to avoid anything controversial. Especially if the subject is employee problems. Don't discipline or fire anybody—just make them do the job.

Maybe your supervisor knows your job so well that she regularly bypasses you and goes directly to your employees with assignments and information. Your employees quickly learn not to trust anything you say or take any of your work assignments seriously because your own supervisor is likely to change them anyway.

Or maybe you have an angry, silent supervisor. You never know whether the problem is with you or someone or something else. You live in fear because any step may turn out to be the wrong one. Just try to get some guidance or information!

## Worklife Nightmares

Worklife itself can offer you miscellaneous nightmares. For example, you know you can't get the work of your department done without the willing and voluntary cooperation of other departments—purchasing, for example. But every time you ask for a necessary favor, you get a total lack of support. (Of course, wait until they need something from you!)

How about the grapevine? Your organization may be filled with rumor after rumor. Are we going to be sold? Is there a layoff on the horizon? Even though the rumors may have nothing to them, work comes to a standstill each time a new wave hits.

Or maybe the nightmare is shifting priorities. Every day (sometimes it seems like every hour), the word comes down that the goalposts have been moved. You get started on Project A and before you really get much accomplished, Project A is overtaken by events and Project B becomes your new priority. For a while.

## Miscellaneous "Environmental" Nightmares

The German philosopher Göethe reminds us, "You must be the hammer or the anvil." Unless, of course, you're in middle management. That's the layer in between the hammer and the anvil.

Front-line supervisors live in a basically untenable position. You are the representative of management to staff, as well as the representative of staff to management. Daily you communicate both up and down the organization, frequently carrying messages no one wants to hear. This leads to the "shoot the messenger" syndrome, in which you take the heat for something you didn't cause merely because you bring the news.

You also have to deal on a daily basis with personalities—those of your staff and your own management, plus those of customers and people in other departments. People seldom check their personalities at the door when they punch in on the time clock. Their personality styles, personal stresses, homelife issues, professional goals, attitudes toward the company, reactions to authority figures, and everything else all become part of your terrain.

Further, you normally don't get authority commensurate with your responsibility. Certainly that's true in the official organization. Savvy supervisors quickly learn, though, that unofficial authority is at least as important as the official variety. Your communications skills, your personal reputation for quality and hard work, your ability to negotiate, your networking success, all have a direct bearing on your real ability to get the work done.

If you're an old hand at this, you know you frequently don't have the people and other resources you feel are necessary to get the work done. Supervisors sometimes suspect senior management sits up late at night thinking of new ways to stick it to their projects or departments. In a way, that's exactly what they do; it's not your imagination.

In every organization, there's always no limit to the useful, desirable work that can be done, but always limited resources with which to do it. Every time management gives you a dollar, a body, or a week to get a job done, that's automatically a dollar, a body, or a week that can't be used for something else. Organizations must work in an atmosphere of resource scarcity in order to accomplish the maximum.

Senior management is often convinced (with good reason) that people hold back from using their full potential. Therefore, they push, assigning "impossible" jobs, knowing from experience that employees frequently get them done anyway. How much work can we really accomplish? We don't know until we reach the point that the work isn't getting done. (This is called the "test to destruction" technique.)

The concept of "fairness" often has little to do with the reality you face as a supervisor. In order to cope with your supervisory nightmares, you need to start with what is now the situation and decide how you will cope with it. The next chapter will explore a survival plan.

# Developing a Survival Plan for Supervisory Nightmares

The majority of supervisory nightmares are solvable, or at least manageable, if you apply the right strategy. While a general strategy necessarily has to be adapted to specific situations, the basic approach is the same for most nightmares. Here's the sequence:

1. Diagnose the situation in behavioral terms.

2. Recognize and deal with your contributions to the problem.

3. Face the problem head on (communicate!).

4. Make a plan.

5. Decide what to do if the plan doesn't work.

## Diagnose the Situation in Behavioral Terms

What *exactly* is going on? By the time a problem has earned "nightmare" status, you may be feeling anger, guilt, and/or frustration, but you need to take a clear, dispassionate look at things. The key is to describe the situation in objective, or "behavioral," terms. Often we tend to define problems by assigning causes and describing those causes, which creates instead a "judgmental" approach.

For example, imagine that you have witnessed an automobile accident. The police officer at the scene asks you what you saw. Would you say, "Well, the driver of the red car was irritated by the heavy traffic and deliberately ran that stoplight"? You wouldn't, because you don't know. Doing so would constitute a judgmental approach, and you don't have enough data to make such a statement. In other words, you might be right or you might be wrong about the motives you impute to the driver of the red car—but on what basis can you be sure?

You probably would answer the officer more along the following lines: "The red car came from the left lane, ran through the red light just as it turned, then skidded into the rear of the green car." That's a simple description of behavior rather than intent (your judgment). "Behavioral" language describes only what you can observe.

The judgmental approach assumes you already know the underlying cause of the behavior. "My friend is jealous of my success." "That person is deliberately trying to manipulate me." Not only might you be wrong, but such judgments will only provoke argument and conflict in trying to resolve the problems, even if you are right.

One of the key principles of supervisory effectiveness, or indeed of communications effectiveness, is that if you can't describe a problem in behavioral terms, you're really unlikely to get any change. Take a few minutes to try the following exercise.

# Exercise:
## *Behavioral Language*

Write down a supervisory nightmare you are currently experiencing.

_____

_____

_____

_____

_____

_____

_____

_____

_____

Now go through your written description looking for judgmental language (language that presupposes you know reasons or motives) and change it to descriptive language (language describing what you observe behaviorally that suggests there is a problem). Be as specific as you can.

1. Judgmental Language _____

   Behavior You Actually Observe _____

2. Judgmental Language _____

   Behavior You Actually Observe _____

3. Judgmental Language _____

   Behavior You Actually Observe _____

4. Judgmental Language _____

   Behavior You Actually Observe _____

5. Judgmental Language _____

   Behavior You Actually Observe _____

# Recognize and Deal With Your Contributions to the Problem

No nightmare situation is ever completely one-sided; you always make a contribution to the problem. This doesn't mean you have done anything wrong—only that perhaps there are steps and actions you could take that you haven't yet. In addition, remember that contributions aren't all negative. Being proactive is making a contribution.

For example, if your issue is supervising friends, you might try some or all of the following steps:

- *Go ahead and let your friends know that you're uncomfortable and you suspect they may be too.* Change in the structure of a relationship is always tough.

- *Tell them about your goals as a supervisor* (e.g., fair treatment with no favoritism, meeting company and departmental goals, and having a positive and professional attitude about work).

- *Encourage them to come to you with feedback about your supervisory style.* And when they do, listen. You may be someone's superior in a work setting, but we're all equals as people.

- *Set up a meeting with the affected people at the beginning of the new supervisory situation—before things have a chance to turn into problems.* Ask for their cooperation; don't just tell them.

Sometimes you can contribute to a problem without even noticing what you're doing. For example, perhaps you didn't start a situation, but your frustration and annoyance is having a feedback effect on the other person. Maybe you feel unwilling to make the first move because he or she is primarily at fault.

One of the difficult parts of being a supervisor is that you're expected to behave better than everybody else. That's true if the problem is with someone on your team but also if it's with your manager. Even if the problem turns out to be 90 percent the other person's fault, you'll often find that others focus far more on your 10 percent share. You have to go first, dealing with your contribution as a first step in achieving change.

Keeping in mind the supervisory nightmare you depicted in the previous exercise, complete the questions in this next one.

# Exercise:
## *My Contributions to the Nightmare*

1. What steps could I take to gain more influence over the situation?

_____

_____

_____

_____

_____

_____

_____

_____

_____

2. What emotions am I experiencing because of the situation, and how might they be affecting the other people involved?

_____

_____

_____

_____

_____

_____

_____

_____

_____

_____

# Face the Problem Head On (Communicate!)

Many situation comedies at some point offer the same plot: One of the lead characters has to say something difficult or unpleasant to another. Because the character doesn't want to offend the other person, he or she tries a series of indirect routes, all of which result in trouble far greater than just getting the situation out in the open in the first place. Confronting other people with a problem may be hard, even painful, but the alternative is always worse.

One powerful approach is "GREAT" for this purpose. It involves establishing the following:

- **G**oals

- **R**oles

- **E**xpectations

- **A**bilities

- **T**ime

If you plan how you will face the problem by looking at each step of the "GREAT" model, you'll be far more prepared and able to resolve your nightmare.

**G**oals. Set goals for the relationship. Discuss how the other person's job fits the current goals of the department, as well as any new goals you want to set. If there's already a problem, such as late delivery of the monthly report, then talk about that specifically. Link the importance of on-time delivery to departmental goals. What are the steps that would need to be taken to ensure timely completion? What obstacles might stand in the way? How might those obstacles be overcome? You want the conversation to revolve around real issues, not personalities.

**R**oles. The question here is how you want to define the roles between yourself and the other person(s). Using the earlier example of a friend supervising a friend, notice that part of the problem is you have two separate roles that appear to be in conflict: friend and employee. You don't want to give up the friendship, but you have obligations as a supervisor that must be met. Start with your ideas about the two sets of roles and how you would ideally have them work. Then write them in behavioral language—language that is observable and measurable. Be prepared to discuss and negotiate to find a mutually acceptable outcome.

**Expectations.** To get what you want, you must first make clear what you want. Even motivated and willing employees can't very well do something for you if they don't know you want it. (The number one problem in communications is the belief that others can read our minds.) If you haven't told them, you'd better assume they don't know. What are your expectations for satisfactory performance? For outstanding performance? Are your expectations different from what the previous supervisor wanted? How do you expect to be treated? How do you expect a good employee to act when there's a problem getting the work done by deadline? Again, describe expectations in behavioral terms. Statements such as "I want you to respect me," or "I want you to treat me like a human being," though certainly good goals, present judgmental language, not behavioral. How would someone *behave* if they respect you? One step might be that if they have to disagree with you, they should do it in private, not in public.

**Abilities.** Employee problems come in three varieties: "Don't Know," "Can't Do," or "Won't Do." To solve any employee problem, you must learn whether the employee has the ability to do the work and, if so, why performance isn't up to par.

Let's look at each of these types of problems in more detail:

1. They *don't know* what you want.

   Solution: Tell them clearly; get feedback.

2. They *can't do* what you want.

   Solution: Training, possibly job redesign, better/appropriate tools to do the job, occasionally reassignment or termination.

3. They *won't do* what you want.

   Next step: Discover the reason:

   - Performance is punished.

   - Failure is rewarded.

   - Performance doesn't matter.

   Solution: Change the rewards and punishments to change the behavior.

"Don't know" problems happen when employees don't know either what is expected or that what they're doing isn't appropriate. To solve a "don't know" problem, people need feedback.

"Can't do" problems occur when the employee lacks the ability to do the work. At issue could be training, the job itself, the tools or resources to do the job, or the person's aptitude for the particular job. To solve a "can't do" problem, people need training, coaching, mentoring, proper tools and equipment—and basic ability. Sometimes even with training and tools a willing employee can't do the job the way it needs to be done. He or she might need to be reassigned, to have duties shifted, or even (occasionally) to be terminated. The test for a "can't do" problem is to ask, "Could the person do the task if I gave him or her $10 million?" If the answer is "yes," then it's not a "can't do."

"Won't do" problems crop up when the employee has the knowledge and the ability but still doesn't perform. There are three possible "won't do" issues: employees perceive they are punished if they do good work (more piled on, given harder assignments), employees perceive they are rewarded if they do bad work (taken off difficult jobs, given more pleasant assignments, have less stress), or employees perceive performance doesn't matter (same salary increase, work conditions, promotion possibilities regardless). To change "won't do" behavior, you must change the underlying rewards and punishments so they reflect your goals.

Make sure that at the beginning of your new relationships, you establish employees' abilities. If you do this together, you get a fairer and more accurate assessment, plus you can begin any needed intervention earlier. If you haven't done this and now face a performance issue, go back and do the assessment together before you try to work out the improvement plan together.

**T**ime. What is your timetable for the desired improvement or the completion of the goal? While some changes need to be made instantly—no profanity in the workplace, for example—others necessarily take longer. If you have an employee who doesn't currently possess the skills to do the work, how fast can you expect him or her to develop them? What assistance can you provide? Can the improvement be made in stages? If so, by when do you expect some initial stages to be achieved?

Following the "GREAT" model doesn't guarantee that you'll end up getting everything you planned. The important element in this process is to make sure the issues are clearly shared. Listen carefully and consider the employee's point of view (though this doesn't mean you have to agree or give in); only by understanding can you reasonably expect to be understood in turn. Express your concerns and problems in behavioral, not judgmental, language. If you have trouble doing this, take time before the meeting to write down what you want to say and analyze it. The following exercise will help.

# Exercise:
## *Prepare to Have GREAT Communication*

**Step 1:** Write a behavioral description of the problem.

_____

_____

_____

_____

_____

_____

_____

_____

_____

**Step 2:** Decide how you plan to approach each element of G-R-E-A-T.

- **Goals:** What is the behavioral goal or goals you would like to achieve? How would things be different if you got the change you wanted? What are the reasons you want or need to achieve these goals?

_____

_____

_____

_____

_____

_____

_____

_____

- **Roles:** What are the roles you want to play and have the other person play in your work situation? (Check that they are defined in behavioral terms.)

My Role                                      Their Role

_____          _____

_____          _____

_____          _____

_____          _____

_____          _____

_____          _____

- **Expectations:** What are your expectations for satisfactory performance? For outstanding performance? Have expectations changed from previous situations? How do you expect to be treated? How do you expect a good employee to act when there is a problem?

_____

_____

_____

_____

_____

- **Abilities:** Is the problem a "Don't Know, "Can't Do," or "Won't Do"? (Always assume it's a "Don't Know" first, then escalate—you'll be more successful that way.)

  ☐ **Don't Know:** How can I best give the information or instruction in behavioral terms?

_____

_____

_____

_____

_____

☐ **Can't Do:** Could the employee do the job for $10 million?

☐ Yes ☐ No

If not, it's a "can't do" problem. What steps could you take to help the employee become able to do the job?

- Training: _____

- Changes in the job structure: _____

_____

- Tools and resources: _____

_____

- Reassignment:_____

_____

☐ **Won't Do:** What are the rewards and punishments (from the team member's point of view) for refusing to do the job the way it needs to be done?

- Performance is punished (list negative consequences of doing the job correctly):

_____

_____

_____

_____

_____

- Failure is rewarded (list positive consequences of not doing the job correctly):

_____

_____

_____

_____

_____

• Performance doesn't matter (why not?):

_____

_____

_____

_____

List ways you can change the rewards and punishments to achieve the desired behavioral change.

• **Time:** What is your timetable? Is this an "instantaneous change" situation or one calling for gradual, steady improvement? What support will you provide? How will you measure progress toward the goal?

_____

_____

_____

_____

_____

The G-R-E-A-T model is a strong initial approach. In this stage, you may need to use the Negative Feedback Model to tell your team member in a positive yet clear manner what needs to be changed.

## Five Steps for Effective Negative Feedback

1. Define the problem in behavioral terms.

2. Relate the impact and your feelings.

3. Ask—then *listen!*—for the real problem.

4. Work out a win/win change.

5. Focus on the positive elements of the relationship.

# Five Steps for Effective Negative Feedback

When we get stressed, we often think less effectively. Supervisory nightmares are normally stress-producers—especially when the solution involves giving negative feedback. We may fear anger, a lack of cooperation, or even revenge-seeking. The solution is to make a plan before you confront. The Negative Feedback Model is a tool before you plan your approach and arrive at a workable solution that both you and the other person can live with. It's a step-by-step approach to giving effective negative feedback in a way that makes it easy for the other person to accept. To use this model, follow the steps in a linear order. Make sure each element is complete before you move on to the next. Be clear in your own mind what you want the outcome to be.

1. **Define the problem in behavioral terms.** Use clear behavioral language to talk about what you observed. Be specific and share as many details as you can. Be calm and talk honestly and openly about your observations.

2. **Relate the impact and your feelings.** Describe the impact of the behavior, both on yourself and on others. Impact can be external (interfered with work) or internal (emotional). You need to describe both elements. When you describe your feelings, make sure you state them as "I" messages (e.g., "When you check each step of the work as I do it, *I feel* that I'm not trusted," as opposed to, "When you micromanage everything I do, *you show* you don't trust me."

3. **Ask—then *listen!*—for the real problem.** Allow the other person to talk about the situation from his or her point of view. Sometimes, people need to make excuses or vent their feelings before they can accept the necessity for change. Let them. You can listen to others and accept their feelings without necessarily agreeing with them. This is also the only way you can find out the reasons or motives for the behavior. Help your friend take responsibility so he or she can learn from the event. Be careful not to turn the person into a victim—he or she has made a mistake. Take for granted the person's desire to correct the mistake. Avoid questions that begin "Why?" or closed-ended questions (those that elicit a "yes" or "no" answer). These only cause defensiveness. Instead, ask questions like, "What were you hoping to achieve?" or "What did you intend when you did that?"

4. **Work out a win/win change.** Negotiate next steps to be taken and write them down together. What are actions you can both agree on? Build on your friend's strengths. Look for choices that will correct the problem, both now and in the future. Make sure planned steps are written in behavioral, observable, and measurable terms.

5. **Focus on the positive elements of the relationship.** Negative feedback, no matter how well it's expressed or how carefully you try to phrase it, is difficult for most people to take. None of us enjoy being told we're wrong, imperfect, out of line, or incompetent—especially when we may suspect we are. Many people take criticism to heart and believe the relationship is permanently damaged as a result of the negative feedback. You need to overcome this tendency by focusing on honest, legitimate positives.

In addition, you need to remember that people are more likely to make the change if they feel they can succeed, and/or if there is a potential positive outcome for them. For example, a person is unlikely to try to change if he or she doesn't feel you'll allow the change, or if he or she can't possibly recover your good opinion. End with a positive comment. State your belief that the person can handle the situation. Help the person receiving the feedback to feel as good as possible. These steps help the employee believe that good results are possible—both for him– or herself as well as for the department. Of course, you can't lie, sugarcoat, or be hypocritical in your positive comment. It must be sincere, congruent, and honest. One more reason to plan your approach before having the dialogue is to give you a chance to identity honest positives.

You may be surprised that simply clearing the air can make many seemingly intractable problems vanish on the spot. Of course, that doesn't always happen. Sometimes you find yourself in an impasse. What then?

Make sure you understand the goals and expectations of the other person (whether or not you agree), and try brainstorming. What options are possible? Expand the number of options, writing each one down without judging quality. In brainstorming, good ideas often piggyback on bad ones, so emphasize quantity of ideas over quality. You may even need to schedule a follow-up meeting to consider the ideas and to add others.

For example, perhaps the problem with the monthly report is that the employee responsible has too many other priorities. You might be able to smooth out the workload and shift priorities, or you might brainstorm ways to make it easier to gather and format information for the report (some software, for instance, may simplify the process). Don't look for your solution only within a narrow range.

The bottom line here is to make a plan before you communicate. When facing the person associated with the problem, you may be nervous or insecure. Having an outline of issues and responses can do a great deal for your personal effectiveness.

## Make a Plan

Most supervisory nightmares didn't start overnight and won't go away overnight, even if you do everything right. Facing the problem and the person is a powerful first step. To make this confrontation a success, you need to end with a plan as well as begin with one. What will the other person do? What will you do? What is the timetable for change? How will you measure whether the change is taking place? What will you do as a next step if the planned change doesn't happen?

A good plan always requires follow-up. If you omit this step, people frequently lose focus. Even if you and they are both motivated to solve the problem, without regular follow-up the desire to solve the problem often gets lost in the day-to-day pressures of the workplace.

By doing the preceding exercises, and discussing their content with the affected person, you can negotiate a satisfactory outcome. Write your plan in the form of a memo (handwritten notes may even be preferable, as the physical act of typing something often makes it seem more serious than it is), and make sure you follow up.

## Decide What to Do If the Plan Doesn't Work

Life is often tough enough without borrowing extra trouble, so don't feel compelled to plan out this part until you have to. The truth is, most nightmares start to become controllable once you face the issue assertively. Let's assume this is one of the other cases, though. What steps can you take?

**Review the results of the previous dialogues.** What happened? Go back to your original plan and review where the breakdown occurred. Readdress that area. Sometimes you'll find that one round isn't enough; you may have to cover exactly the same ground two or three (or five) times before you get the change you need.

**Provide clear and consistent supervision.** If you can establish measurement of satisfactory work, do so. Give specific deadlines for all assignments (no "ASAP" or "do it when you get around to it"), note the due dates in your own calendar, and check to make sure you receive the work on time. Ask specific questions on work progress.

Link the improvements you require to strategic and performance goals of the department or organization, or to the employee's own performance appraisal process. One part of the belief that "performance doesn't matter" is that the desired performance is not linked to any greater goal.

People naturally look to your behavior, not your words, to determine what's really important in your department. When it seems hard to crack down on one employee's lack of performance, remember that if you don't, everyone else will conclude that's the appropriate work performance level. Your problems will multiply.

**Work on the interpersonal issues.** You may want to set up more regular sessions for feedback and relating, rather than waiting to meet only when things go wrong. Depending on the severity of the nightmare, these could become development conferences that provide help for both you and the "problem" person.

**Have a formal development conference.** Clearly assess the natural strengths and development needs of the employee. It may be time for a reassignment or adjustment of duties, and your situation may have been the catalyst for that realization. Remember, sometimes people "act out" because they need help for something they're not consciously aware of. If you include employees in the diagnosis and discovery, their ownership leads to better acceptance. As before, make sure this process emphasizes individual behavioral, not judgmental, language. And don't forget to link individual goals to departmental and organizational goals.

**If you're to the point of formal discipline, get help.** You may find yourself in a position where disciplinary action is necessary. If you suspect things are getting to that point, talk to your supervisor and personnel officer before you need to take action. Often their more distant perspective can help you identify options you might have overlooked. They also may have the power to institute solutions beyond your authority, such as transferring an otherwise valuable employee who just can't adapt to your supervisory role.

Finally, assess any political issues, especially if the person is not your employee, or is your employee but has seniority and wide contacts in the organization. If your battle extends into the office politics arena, make sure you're aware of the unofficial agenda as well as the official one.

# Bearing the Emotional Burden of Supervisory Nightmares

Randy Newman wrote (and Frank Sinatra sang), "It's lonely at the top." Supervisors frequently report feelings of isolation. You're not "one of the gang" any more. Former co-workers won't share the same gossip with you, and they certainly won't invite you to their let's-gripe-about-our-rotten-boss sessions!

The emotional burden of supervision results from a variety of factors. Perhaps you have experienced some of the following:

- Feelings of emotional separation from old team members and previous "work friends"

- Feelings of having to support management decisions that you personally disagree with

- Feelings that you can't be candid and honest with team members and others

- Feelings of being whipsawed between management and your team members

- Feelings of being disliked or resented because of the position you hold

- Feelings of being underpaid and under-empowered for the responsibilities you have

While other supervisors are in the same emotional boat as you, you'll seldom find the same solidarity at this level as among staff. You're in different departments, you work with different people all day, and you may be more competitive with one another than staff would be. You don't have the same opportunities to vent and let off steam about your emotional frustrations as staff members have.

So what do you do? Individual supervisors have successfully coped with the emotional burdens in a variety of ways. Try using more than one of the following techniques as they apply to your situation.

1. Don't take it personally.

2. List your payoffs.

3. Manage your stress effectively.

4. Measure your problems.

5. Talk with someone trustworthy.

6. Work on your skills.

7. Care about people and work.

## Don't Take It Personally

Sometimes you may feel that the entire world (or at least your entire organization) hates you. Sometimes that ill will is rather directly expressed. It's human nature to want to be liked, and for some supervisors the feeling of no longer being so is a major cause of pain and pressure in their work role.

The unfortunate truth is, you may not be as popular as you were in your presupervisory days. Your role as a supervisor often includes carrying some negative emotional baggage. Although it's difficult not to take this personally, you must avoid doing so, because the truth is, it really *isn't* personal.

There are three important principles to keep in mind here.

1. **Nobody at work likes you—or dislikes you, either.** Although this may be difficult to accept, it's usually true—because your team members seldom know the real "you." When people go to work, they usually adopt work behaviors and take on work roles, which in turn form a "work mask." People react to you based on that mask, not your innate personality. Many new supervisors are shocked when their previous colleagues say, "You've changed." You may not feel that change inside, but it's nevertheless real. When you change your responsibilities and level of authority, your "work mask" necessarily changes, and therefore so do others' experience of you. The fact that the change is mostly external, not internal, makes it no less real.

    Take some time to reflect on your own need to be liked. Although almost everybody wants to be liked, some people actually *need* it. If this applies to you, it can create problems, since sometimes as a supervisor you must make decisions and choices that run afoul of somebody's preferences.

    The paradox about wanting to be liked as a supervisor is that the actions you would expect to help you meet that goal (giving in to employee demands, accepting substandard work without complaint, doing something yourself rather than asking somebody else to take it on) actually have a different effect: you become disrespected and patronized, albeit in a friendly way.

    The supervisors who end up being liked best by their staff are also the ones who are effective in their supervisory role: professional, work-oriented, consistent, fair, honest, and assertive. They are respected.

    Although it seems paradoxical, if you really want to be liked, work at earning respect first. When combined with good people skills and respect for others, such efforts provide the ingredients for real friendship from others. If the goal of being liked turns you into a doormat instead, remember: Nobody cares about a doormat one way or another.

2. **People don't react to you as your behavior has earned.** Many team members have a mental box marked "Supervisor," and when you become one, they put you in that box. You may be very surprised at how people treat you—perhaps with hostility, suspicion, resentment, and even fear that doesn't seem to have any justification in your own behavior. This is, sadly, normal. When you enter the "supervisor" box, you're treated as a combination of what your own behavior has earned, plus people's previous experiences with supervisors, plus their feelings about the overall organization, plus, in some cases, leftover problems from Mommy or Daddy. All of that baggage shows up in the supervisor/team member relationship.

3. **People may see you as a threat—and you are.** Imagine for a minute that you're in a room with another person and he or she has a loaded gun. You are unarmed. Wouldn't you tend to feel a bit nervous? You may know the person and know he or she has no actual intent of shooting you, but you're aware of the gun and of the threat it could pose. The military defines "threat" not as the intention of some enemy to hurt us, but rather as the potential of that enemy to hurt us.

The moment you become a supervisor, you have at least the theoretical power to fire other people. You can give them rotten job assignments, offer poor performance appraisals, sabotage their ability to get promoted, bad-mouth them to senior management, and even ruin their career. Although you harbor no malicious intention to do anyone harm, you still have the power. When you become a supervisor, it's as if someone strapped a loaded gun to you. You're packing heat. You have become a threat, and others can't regard you the same way they did before you got the power.

# List Your Payoffs

Some people are volunteers in the army of supervisors; others come in as draftees. Ultimately, however, few people are ever completely successful doing what they truly hate. That is, if you find your role as a supervisor more and more a source of unhappiness, you need to follow the classic advice of success, "Do what you intrinsically enjoy, learn to enjoy what you do, or get out." It's possible that you aren't emotionally well suited for the role of supervisor, in which case your best solution is to change positions and return to the nonsupervisory ranks.

Most commonly, a person becomes a supervisor looking for certain payoffs, sometimes finding that the problems overwhelm the payoffs or that the payoffs anticipated don't seem to exist. If you're not receiving the payoffs you want and need from being a supervisor, then you must take the initiative to get them. Use the following exercise to develop an action plan to improve your own payoffs.

# Exercise:
## *Why Supervise?*

Circle "Y" for "Yes" or "N" for "No." My payoffs for being a supervisor include:

**Y  N  Making more money.**

If this is one of your supervisory payoffs, you may be disappointed, at least at the first-level rank. Initially, supervisors usually get a little more pay for a lot more responsibility. At higher levels, the financial payoff is likely to be greater. If money is your main goal, is this the best route to get it? What steps can you take to improve your financial rewards?

**Possible Action Steps:**

1. Find out about bonus or merit pay opportunities.

2. Negotiate for a raise, either now or after achieving a certain objective.

3. Determine what others with similar responsibilities are making.

4. Understand the financial situation of your organization.

5. Get training and developmental assignments to increase your skills—and your worth.

*Add your own steps:*

6. _____

7. _____

8. _____

**Y  N  Having more influence and power over people.**

Although we're not "supposed" to enjoy power for its own sake, the truth is that many people do. There isn't necessarily anything wrong with that unless the power is used in destructive or harmful ways. Power and authority can operate constructively, to focus attention on key problems and issues, to motivate people to achieve more, and to help others in their personal and professional growth. If this is a goal, you may be frustrated when people don't seem to respect your supervisory authority, or don't do what you need them to do, or don't value your attempts to help them. Remember, influence and power over others requires their consent. Ultimately, you must develop a relationship of mutual consensual development with your employees. What steps can you take to develop your leadership skills, to earn respect and obedience from others, or to influence people toward your goals?

**Possible Action Steps:**

1. Get training in leadership/motivational skills.

2. Get feedback from team members about your leadership effectiveness.

3. Get feedback from your management about your leadership effectiveness.

*Add your own steps:*

4. _____

5. _____

6. _____

**Y  N  Having more control over work situations.**

A powerful reason for seeking management authority is to have more control over work situations. You may have been frustrated at the direction of your department or of the corporate mission. You may have felt that management was not doing the right thing. Now you're in a position of authority and control and seek to use your position to make changes and achieve control. Instead, you find yourself being fought in all directions—by staff and by management. The status quo has substantial inertia, and change always is harder and slower than you expect. What could you do to increase your legitimate control?

**Possible Action Steps:**

1. Volunteer for committee/task force assignments that might increase your influence.

2. List the changes you think should be made, rank them by order of desirability/difficulty, and start by working toward one single change.

3. Read management books on the topics of your concern and look for strategies that might help.

4. Build relationships with key managers to increase your influence.

*Add your own steps:*

5. _____

6. _____

7. _____

**Y  N  Being included more in the process.**

A high need for inclusion motivates some people to seek supervisory responsibilities: to be part of the process, to be asked, to be part of the decisions, to be part of the group that counts. Yet does it seem that every time you turn around, you discover meetings you weren't invited to, decisions made behind your back, and people who seemingly want to "include you out"? What steps can you take to increase your inclusion?

**Possible Action Steps:**

1. Study networking techniques and develop a plan to build better relationships.

2. Ask others about their duties, responsibilities, and goals, and ask how you can help them.

3. Get feedback from trusted associates about how your personality affects your ability to be included.

4. Volunteer for committees and special project team assignments.

5. Join trade and industry associations to increase your range of contacts.

*Add your own steps:*

6. _____

7. _____

8. _____

**Y  N  Improving long-term career opportunities.**

Even if immediate financial rewards aren't very great, the long-term potential in a supervisory position may be substantial. Unfortunately, you may find yourself so deeply immersed in unsolvable problems and no-win situations that you wonder if you were set up to fail. It's important to remember that you can't delegate responsibility for your career growth; you must plan and act. What can you do to increase your long-term career opportunities?

**Possible Action Steps:**

1. Seek out training opportunities both inside and outside the organization.

2. Consider enrolling in after-hours or weekend graduate studies.

3. Ask for developmental assignments to increase your long-term worth to the organization.

4. Get feedback on your strengths and weaknesses and develop plans for personal and professional improvement.

5. Get involved in trade and industry organizations.

*Add your own steps:*

6. _____

7. _____

8. _____

**Y N**  **Expanding and improving my professional skills.**

Many supervisors not only are motivated by money and career growth, but also by the opportunity to develop new skills. Unfortunately, you may find yourself stuck doing the same things over and over again because you're the most experienced and technically capable member of your own team. What can you do to improve and expand your professional skills?

**Possible Action Steps:**

1. Work on your delegation skills—help your team grow by asking them to take on more of your previous responsibilities.

2. Look for training and development opportunities both for yourself and for your team members.

3. Seek out new work assignments that stretch you in new directions.

4. Remind your managers about your range of skills so you'll get opportunities in new areas.

*Add your own steps:*

5. _____

6. _____

7. _____

**Additional Payoffs**

The more individual payoffs you can list, the more energy you can focus on becoming a more effective supervisor.

**My additional payoffs for supervising are:**

_____

_____

_____

_____

_____

**Possible Action Steps for Each Payoff:**

1. _____

2. _____

3. _____

4. _____

5. _____

6. _____

7. _____

8. _____

9. _____

10. _____

## Manage Your Stress Effectively

Stress comes with the territory of being a supervisor. While it's impossible to eliminate all the stress from your work life, you can—and must—reduce it in order to cope with the tough situations in which you find yourself.

Even worse, in addition to its personal toll, the symptoms of stress start to send messages to the people around you. They begin to worry about your effectiveness. However, you shouldn't pretend to be invulnerable. Recent management studies suggest that showing some stress and anger in appropriate ways can actually improve your effectiveness as a supervisor. The key word here is "appropriate."

How much stress is too much?

One of the core principles in knowing when you are overloaded is to develop your own personal "stress barometer." What tells you when it's all getting to be too much? Is it when all the other drivers on the road start being incompetent? Is it when all you can think about each day is what you plan to do with Ed McMahon's ten million dollars when you win? Is it when you start believing that the random slights and insults of everyday life are all personal? Is it disrupted sleep, or other symptoms of depression? Listing some personal stress barometers in the following exercise will warn you before it all gets to be too much.

# Exercise:
## *My Stress Barometer*

1. Think of times when your stress level has become too high. What feelings, physical reactions, or other symptoms did you experience? These can be your warning signs for future stress.

_____

_____

_____

_____

_____

_____

_____

_____

_____

2. These are the steps I will take when I feel my stress getting out of control:

_____

_____

_____

_____

_____

_____

_____

_____

_____

There's an old story about a young man who worked in a deli during college. He felt ill-treated by his boss and customers and complained about the unfairness and all his problems. An older man took him aside one evening and said, sympathetically, "You have a lot of problems, don't you?"

"Yeah," the young man replied. "This place is rotten and the boss is a jerk."

With that, the old man rolled up his sleeve. On his arm was an Auschwitz tattoo. He smiled at the young man and said, "I was in a pretty rotten place too. It taught me one thing: to tell the difference between an annoyance and a problem."

You may have many annoyances, but you probably don't have many problems.

Two of the most valuable pieces of stress management advice are "Have reasonable expectations of yourself and others," and "Learn to relax on command."

Perfectionists hold themselves and often others to impossible standards, and thus become doomed to frustration and failure. Perfection is a goal mortals can't attain. You can be good, you can be better, you can even be excellent, but perfect is out of the question. And, if the only way for you to have a good work life is for all those other people around you to suddenly start treating you right, you have a long, lonely wait ahead.

Learn to relax on command. Just as there is a stress reflex, there is also a relaxation counterpart. It can be triggered by methods ranging from biofeedback and medication to counting to ten before opening your mouth. Pick your favorite way to relax and use it.

If your nightmare is getting to the point that you are experiencing poor sleep, loss of appetite, and/or continual tiredness, it's possible that you're slipping into a depression. Depression is the common cold of mental illness. Current studies suggest that roughly 25 percent of the population will suffer from clinical depression at some point in their lives. Depression is a serious condition, but fortunately, it's one the mental health profession is good at treating. See your physician for a physical examination first, since sometimes symptoms of depression can mask an underlying physical ailment; then seek out therapeutic help. There is neither shame nor weakness in getting help.

Finally, develop a good sense of humor. In Robert McGraw's *Learning to Laugh at Work,* he notes, "Being able to see the light side of problems not only helps you survive, it also shows others that you have self-confidence and the ability to stay 'centered' and keep your priorities straight in spite of difficulties. Colleagues will trust you and trust your judgment—people naturally follow a confident leader."

## Measure Your Problems

Psychologically, people tend to perceive negatives more strongly than positives. For example, it takes four compliments to equal the emotional power of a single criticism. Sometimes, therefore, the nightmare situation you perceive may not be as serious as you feel it is.

If the problem is someone who argues with you "every time" you present a work assignment, you might keep a log of work assignments you give that person and the number of times the person actually argues with you. This is worth doing for two reasons: If you can document the pattern, you have much more power to get the person to change, and you may discover that the negative response doesn't occur "every time" after all—only occasionally.

Begin a work journal as a way to track situations and identify patterns. If you do this, though, be careful. Don't write anything in your journal that you wouldn't be comfortable having read aloud in a court of law. (Diaries have a way of being drawn into litigation.) This particular consideration shouldn't scare you off from a valuable technique—just remember to write down observable behavior in nonemotional terms. That is, don't use the journal as a place to vent fears, frustrations, anger, or personal opinions about people's character, habits, or personality quirks. Those are not "facts," but opinions, and could be used to show a pattern of prejudice on your part. What you actually see and witness should be recorded, and you have no reason to be ashamed of or fearful about the truth. A sample Incident Log format is presented on the page 43.

The idea is to try to confirm whether what you suspect is happening actually is, based on your record of the incidents. For example, you might think, "Every time I give Harry a work assignment, he complains." For two weeks, keep track of every time you give Harry a work assignment and how he reacts. At the end of the two weeks, you discover that out of ten work assignments, he complained only twice. Now, those complaints may well have been annoying, but they aren't as constant or as frequent as you thought.

# Incident Log Format

I perceive the following behavior(s) in employee _____ :

| When | What | Impact |
|---|---|---|
|  |  |  |
|  |  |  |
|  |  |  |
|  |  |  |
|  |  |  |

Actual incidence of the behavior(s) over a two-week period:

| Day | Incident Log |
|---|---|
| Day 1 |  |
| Day 2 |  |
| Day 3 |  |
| Day 4 |  |
| Day 5 |  |
| Day 6 |  |
| Day 7 |  |
| Day 8 |  |
| Day 9 |  |
| Day 10 |  |

My perception was:  ☐ Confirmed
by the Incident Log    ☐ Not confirmed
by the Incident Log

*Bearing the Emotional Burden of Supervisory Nightmares*

## Talk With Someone Trustworthy

Two of the jobs with the lowest life expectancy are Iron Man and Super Woman. The fact that it's difficult to find someone to lean on about the stress and emotional burdens that come with supervision doesn't mean it's impossible. A trusted work confidant (not one of your own team members), a close professional friend, even your boss or mentor (depending on your relationship) may be someone you can go to with problems.

The best way to approach this is as follows:

- Don't overburden any single person with your problems.

- Focus on solutions, not problems.

- Be willing to listen and appreciate advice and counsel, even if you decide not to use it.

- Limit emotional venting—but a little bit is okay.

- Don't share confidential information about someone else unless the person you're confiding in has a professional need to know about it (e.g., your boss or an HR department representative).

- Provide listening, emotional support, and constructive advice in return.

- Be sincerely grateful and show it.

It may be "lonely at the top," but you can get reasonable amounts of support if you try.

## Work on Your Skills

Becoming a supervisor isn't a promotion—it's a career change. You move from an orientation around facts and tasks to a new one centered on people and systems. Your problems change from short-term to long-range, from solvable to at best manageable. You move from clear to fuzzy, from known to unknown, from performance to responsibility for performance. Your job becomes not just quantitatively different but qualitatively different as well.

Part of what got you promoted to supervisory rank in the first place was your skill at the work you did. Now you need to focus on learning and developing supervisory skills. How to motivate, how to delegate, how to negotiate, how to plan, how to work with different personalities—these are the areas you need to prosper in for the rest of your career. Make the commitment to lifelong learning as a supervisor. Improving your skills will help you solve some of your nightmares while making you feel more confident and more able.

## Care About People and Work

Those around you quickly form an opinion about how much you care about them, their needs, and their interests. Supervisors frequently get better treatment if they show genuine, unforced interest in the lives and goals of their employees. Supervisors also get better treatment if they show genuine caring about the organizational mission and goals, and about the quality of products and services.

Every supervisor is a role model, and those around you take their cues about how hard they should work and how much they should care from your personal attitude. If you aren't getting the performance from other people, sometimes it's because you don't show the empathy, passion, and commitment in your own behavior. Caring is part of your job description, and it's a requirement for long-term success.

# How to Cope With Employee Nightmares

# What Is an Employee Nightmare?

The "Pareto Principle," also known as the "80-20" rule, suggests that 80 percent of your team gives you about 20 percent of your supervisory problems, and 20 percent gives you the remaining 80 percent. It's usually the case that only a few team members will present serious problems, and only a few of those escalate all the way into the "nightmare" zone.

An employee nightmare, as opposed to a normal employee problem, often occurs when a problem turns personal. Someone may resent your move into a position of authority or dislike the perceived change in your behavior. Perhaps a team member harbors a resentment toward your organization as a whole.

If a staff problem has a personal dimension, it's not necessarily true that your behavior has been at fault—although it is possible that you have contributed to the situation. Some people have a basic difficulty with authority figures wherever they see them. Others may have a stylistic conflict with you, and dislike your natural way of doing things.

Employee nightmares are often about power. You have official power, but that's never as much as you need. Employees have power too. Supervisors realize sooner or later that staff members have the power to ruin their career and get them fired—if the members really put their minds to it. You cannot take this power away from people; you can only behave in a way that keeps them from using it.

It's uncomfortable for someone to feel they are in a subordinate position. Some employees don't like having a boss; they don't like being told what to do. They discover that if they push, they end up with greater latitude, because the supervisor doesn't always enforce his or her authority.

Should you enforce your authority? Think of supervision like parenting. It's important that parents make clear the authority they possess. Children naturally push against that limit, and if parents allow the battle to turn exclusively on the issue of who has the power, they end up in a never-ending war. Effective parents set some absolute boundaries and negotiate the rest, and don't take it personally when a child challenges the boundaries. Taking the time to explain the reasons why you must insist on a certain way, offering to discuss options with employees as long as they achieve the necessary departmental goals, compromising when it doesn't ultimately matter to the department—all are ways to get others to accept your authority and to work within boundaries.

Finally, employee nightmares sometimes involve your role as representative of the company. Supervisors must sometimes make decisions and take action based on policy decisions created at a higher level and with which they may personally disagree. Supervisors are often caught in the middle, without absolute decision-making power. Supervisors learn to accept a certain amount of ill will and frustration that's actually aimed at the company, even though it's taken out on them.

The chapters that follow look at some specific, common employee nightmares and apply effective techniques to solving—or at least coping with—them.

# Help! I'm Supervising a "Friend"

*Last Thursday she finally turned in the monthly report. It was a week late and my boss had been asking for it, but when I pointed that out, she accused me of becoming "one of them." I felt angry and guilty at the same time, because I used to complain about being overworked and yet I knew the monthly reports had to be done on time.*

*I can't believe the way my so-called "friends" have been treating me since I got promoted. At first everybody seemed glad about it, but as soon as I tried to get people to do their jobs, they ignored me, just as if I weren't really the supervisor. I ask and ask and finally end up doing a lot of the work myself. Even the little bit that they do results in nonstop whining. I really feel victimized.*

*One of my best friends really needed a job and this vacancy sounded ideal for him, but now it looks like our friendship itself is on the line. He's in over his head. Although he can't do the work and admits he has problems, he isn't even trying to do better. Every time I start to take action, he tells me about the problems in his personal life and all the reasons he just has to have this job. If I end up firing him, he'll probably get evicted from his apartment. I just can't do that to him, and besides, our friendship would be destroyed, which really means a lot to me.*

Supervising your friends is a classic recipe for trouble. One recommendation often made is not to do it in the first place, exactly for the reasons illustrated in the preceding examples. You can't always avoid the situation, however. Many times your first supervisory position involves becoming the leader of your current work group. Which means that supervising friends, at least work friends, automatically comes with the territory.

Not all friend/work relationships are poisonous. A friend who respects you and cares about the work may turn out to be one of your very best employees, someone you can trust to give you a straight answer when you need feedback, someone you can assign to a position of responsibility and know you'll end up with a good job.

Sometimes, though, friend/work relationships do turn sour for a variety of reasons, some of them malicious and some purely accidental. Here's how to apply the five-point problem-solving plan discussed in Section 1 to this particular nightmare.

## Diagnose the Situation in Behavioral Terms

What exactly is going on in your situation? (Your problem may or may not resemble the examples that launched this chapter.) What is the history of your friendship? What specifically is the problem? Take an objective and dispassionate look at the situation. If it's reached "nightmare" status, you're probably angry, guilty, and frustrated. The friendship may now be suffering as much because of your attitude as anything else, even if you didn't necessarily initiate the problem. Following are some possible diagnoses that may fit your situation.

**Perceptions of favoritism.** Favoritism—preferring one employee over another for reasons other than work performance—is a common accusation leveled at supervisors. Although sometimes there's some truth in it, the perception often results from misinterpretation. However, don't overlook a third possibility: charging you with playing favorites is a good way to manipulate your behavior.

**Problems in getting good work performance.** When a friend is not performing at a satisfactory level, distinct problems may occur. You may have trouble giving negative feedback to someone with whom you have a personal relationship. The friend may have trouble taking correction from you because outside work, you're equals. Sometimes a friend struggling with the job may be reluctant to ask you for help, fearing you'll lose respect for him or her.

**Negative attitudes about the organization.** Most organizations experience some internal complaining by staff. It's nearly unavoidable, since no company can ever please all employees all the time (even if that were an appropriate strategy to pursue). People have their own ideas about proper corporate behavior, goals and missions, and how much work is appropriate for the pay they receive. Besides, no organization is perfect—some complaining takes aim at real management problems and deficiencies.

Before you became a supervisor, there's a good chance you participated in some of this (you may still), but in a supervisory position, it becomes inappropriate to share negative attitudes with your staff. Suddenly you're outside the group, and suddenly you're "one of *them.*" The hostility and negativity get directed at you because you're closest and you're expected to understand. Not sharing "attitude adjustment sessions" with your friends can put up a distance barrier.

**Perception of manipulation.** You may feel that some of your friends are trying to manipulate your behavior because of your relationship. Your friends may feel you're trying to manipulate them in return. While manipulation can and does happen, all too often we experience the perception without the reality.

Let's say that one of your friends sighs and looks depressed when you give her an unpleasant work assignment. She doesn't actually say anything negative, but the look on her face makes you feel instantly guilty. Is she trying to manipulate you, or is she simply less than thrilled about the work assignment? If your feelings of guilt make you alter your behavior, you will likely feel that your friend has manipulated you, but it was you who chose to behave differently.

# Recognize and Deal With Your Contributions

As soon as you're in a position of supervising friends, address the issue up front, either in a group (if all have been your friends) or one at a time if only one or two are affected. Go ahead and let them know that you're uncomfortable and you suspect they may be too. Change in the structure of a relationship is always tough. Set and share your goals as a supervisor, and ask for the input of your friends to help determine how you might behave in that role. Solicit their support for "all of us doing our jobs" and achieving the department's goals. Encourage them to come to you with feedback about your supervisory style (and when they do, *listen*).

As a supervisor, especially a new one, expect a certain amount of teasing (some barbed) and testing at the beginning of this new relationship—people have to probe to find out what the real limits are (as opposed to the theoretical ones). They also need to explore how they feel about it. It's important to be good natured as this occurs, and equally important to know how and when to draw the line.

Draw the line when comments become nasty and sarcastic, when you are accused of improper behavior (even in a joking manner), when the "joke" accompanies a refusal to follow a legitimate order, when teasing becomes an employee's method of excusing poor performance, or when one or two people continue the teasing for weeks or months after others have accepted the new work relationship.

"Drawing the line" does not mean getting angry, negative, or defensive. Instead, it's an indication that you should deal with the comment seriously rather than ignoring it with a good-natured smile. Always confront the issue in private with the affected party or parties, never in public.

## Face the Problem Head On (Communicate!)

The best time to handle the situation is before it turns into a nightmare—but it may already have become one. To get the change you want, you must confront the problem directly. Direct confrontation doesn't have to be angry or ugly (in fact, it's better if you don't use those approaches): it just has to be direct. Assertive. Clear. And you're entitled.

Use the "GREAT" model from Section 1 to help you develop a communications strategy. When you confront a friend, you may feel nervous or insecure going in. Thus, planning your approach in advance isn't manipulation—it's helpful to both you and the other person. Complete the following exercise as a way to help you prepare.

# Exercise:
## *Friend Nightmare Planning Worksheet*

**Step 1:** Describe the problem with your friend(s) in behavioral terms. (If necessary, first write it in emotional and judgmental language, and then edit it.)

_____

_____

_____

_____

_____

_____

_____

_____

_____

**Step 2:** Decide how you plan to approach each element of G-R-E-A-T.

**Goals:**

_____

_____

_____

_____

_____

_____

_____

_____

_____

_____

_____

**Roles:**

My Role                    Their Role

_____    _____
_____    _____
_____    _____
_____    _____

**Expectations:**

_____
_____
_____
_____
_____
_____

**Abilities:** "Don't Know, "Can't Do," or "Won't Do"?

☐ **Don't Know:**

_____
_____
_____
_____
_____
_____

☐ **Can't Do:**

- Training: _____
- Changes in the job structure: _____
- Tools and resources: _____
- Reassignment or separation: _____

☐ **Won't Do:**

- Reasons:

_____

_____

_____

_____

- How you can change rewards/punishments:

_____

_____

_____

_____

**Time:**

_____

_____

_____

_____

_____

## Make an Action Plan

Write down the steps you and your friend/employee will take as a result of your communication. Make sure the plan includes some things *you* will do (ask, not tell, your friend to do work assignments; give negative feedback only in private; go to lunch together at least once every two weeks and not talk about work; etc.) so that the process isn't exclusively one-way. (Plus, it's easier sometimes to change yourself than it is to change someone else.) Set a follow-up meeting to discuss the efforts you both are making.

In order to cope with some of the specific diagnoses detailed earlier, integrate some of the following suggestions into your communication and action planning:

**Negative attitudes about the organization.** One way to help you cope is to share with your staff the "80-20 Work Rule": No job is perfect. The best job in the world will still include 20 percent that is difficult and unpleasant. If you find that 80 percent of your job is positive and the 20 percent that's unpleasant consists of things you can live with, congratulations! You have a great job! That doesn't mean you won't work to improve some of the distasteful 20 percent; just keep it in perspective.

**Dealing with manipulative behavior.** Assume that your friend/employees are "innocent until proven guilty." These people, like any other employees, will naturally express feelings and attitudes about the work, the environment, and you as a supervisor. If the feelings and attitudes affect you more when they come from your friends, the issue is yours, not theirs.

Occasionally, attempts at manipulation become so overt and obvious you can't mistake them. "Come on—I'm your friend. You don't want to do that to me. Do it to someone else. They don't like you, so give them the rotten work assignment."

If someone tries the direct approach, ask, "What are you trying to accomplish here?" Move the dialogue into the work sphere, not personal territory. Most of the time people back off, because they don't want to actually say that they want to be exempted from their regular work. If your friend does choose to come right out and ask you to play favorites because of your relationship, then you can shift into a problem-solving process focusing on work requirements, which is a completely satisfactory strategy. Now you can face the issue squarely and talk it through.

## Decide What to Do If Dialogue Doesn't Work

How important is the friendship? How serious is the problem? How much of a threat does dealing with the problem pose to the friendship? Is this really a two-way friendship, or is there some pretending going on? You need answers to these questions.

Like any interpersonal relationship, friendships need work and nurturing. You may want to set up more regular sessions for feedback and relating, in which you both can share information and observations to smooth the way, rather than waiting to interact when things go wrong. Depending on the severity of the nightmare, these could become development conferences that provide help for you both.

If you have to crack down on your friend, does that spell the end of your relationship? Possibly, but not necessarily. Sometimes it may be the best thing for the friendship. Sometimes a friend will respect you more and appreciate your integrity for being willing to face up to the issue.

Sometimes, however, your friendship will become a casualty of the supervisory relationship. That's not necessarily the fault of the crackdown; some people have enough difficulty relating to authority that sustaining your friendship will be impossible, regardless of what you do. As the cartoon character "Superchicken" says, "You knew the job was dangerous when you took it."

# Help! I'm Supervising Someone I Passed Over

*You know, the most frustrating thing of all is that she never applied for the job and never even told anyone she wanted it! Now she goes around telling people that I only have the job because I'm such a brown-noser, that I went behind her back, that I cut her down—and none of this is the truth. People naturally seem to want to believe the worst, and now I'm afraid my staff has chosen sides against me.*

*Yes, he has seniority, yes, he has lots of experience, and yes, he's good at the job. He's even better at some of the technical work than I am. But I got promoted because he doesn't have any people skills—he's abrupt, he's patronizing, he loudly tells people how stupid management is. Naturally, he doesn't see it that way. He's starting to be actively insubordinate. I don't want to fire him, but I can't take much more of this.*

*As team leader, she was over her head. She kept doing it all herself, didn't keep people informed, lost her temper several times, and let things get really disorganized. Management should have stepped in earlier, but they didn't, and she felt really humiliated when she was demoted. Now I'm the supervisor, when she had been my boss. She bends my ear every day about how rotten management is and how unfair they are. When things go right, she acts like my situation isn't as hard as hers was, or that I'm not doing as good a job, and she tells other people these things.*

Some people are made supervisors because of their communications and administrative skills, others because of their technical abilities or outstanding work on a major project. Success as a supervisor depends far more on the first group: communications and administrative ability. That's why people of undeniable technical ability are sometimes passed over for supervisory positions, or even demoted after a trial period.

Effective supervisors have to balance the people/administrative skills on the one hand and their technical/job knowledge strengths on the other. Both are important, but 80 percent of your next promotion will depend on the people/administrative side.

There are many sources of potential conflict involving co-workers you've passed over, beaten out, or replaced in supervisory roles. The good news is that supervising people in those situations is not automatically or necessarily a recipe for a supervisory nightmare. You may be fortunate enough to get a staff member who knows that he or she wasn't suited for the supervisory role. If you work at those relationships, you may be fortunate enough to achieve a win/win outcome, in which you and the technically talented staffer can help each other succeed.

When conflicts do arise, however, the by-now familiar five-point strategy offers the best chance of resolution.

## Diagnose the Situation in Behavioral Terms

If you have a supervisory nightmare involving a passed-over employee, the first step is to describe the behavior that is the problem, and then try to identify the reasons for the conflict that now exists. There are several options.

**Need for autonomy and independence.** The passed-over employee sometimes didn't really want the supervisory position in the first place, but didn't want anybody else to have it because of a strong need for autonomy and independence. Rather than a personal problem with you, it's simply a dislike for being told what to do. Employees who are competent and know it often want the freedom to do the job their way, feeling that a supervisor—any supervisor—is an obstacle.

**Feeling of public humiliation or competency challenge.** The passed-over employee may feel threatened, sensing that not getting the supervisory position (or worse, having it taken away) is a negative reflection on his or her competence. If a person feels publicly humiliated or unrecognized, the predictable result is anger, resentment, and acting out.

**Need for power and control.** Why did the passed-over employee want to become a supervisor? Sometimes the issue is his or her desire for power and control. In fact, this may have played some role in why the employee didn't get the job in the first place.

Because interpersonal skills are so critical in any supervisory position, the passed-over employee may have been seen as someone prone to dictatorial behavior or strongly negative interactions. This is especially true if the employee previously had been given team-leader or project-leader assignments.

**Competitive feelings or personal issues.** It may simply be a personal conflict. "I didn't want the job, but I sure didn't want *you* to get it," the employee may be thinking. Competition among employees can be a positive stimulation to productivity, but if one person is promoted and the other is not, the competitive feelings can get out of hand.

You may be contributing to this, especially if you were an active part of the competition. It's nearly impossible not to feel satisfaction when we beat someone in a good, fair race. No matter how well you behave, therefore, the other person can easily feel you're rubbing it in.

**Negative attitudes about the organization.** Certain employees who are otherwise able may keep themselves from advancement by believing that management in your organization is incompetent, wrong-headed, or misguided. If he or she were to become a supervisor, then things would be done right! Because this is a direct criticism of management itself, even the good and positive ideas and talents of this employee may be dismissed.

This becomes a circular process: the employee dislikes management, and management therefore becomes less likely to validate and support the employee. The employee dislikes management more for neglecting him or her, management responds to that dislike, and so forth.

## Recognize and Deal With Your Contributions

You always make some contribution to the nightmare situations in which you find yourself. You might be avoiding a direct confrontation with the employee, either because you fear a poor outcome or desire not to have open conflict. You might be dealing with your own anxieties in your new leadership role and trying to overcontrol others. You might be participating in competitive behavior that was more appropriate when you were both equals.

Take a no-fault approach to this process. You may well have done nothing "wrong," but there may still be more things you can do right.

## Face the Problem Head On (Communicate!)

Complete the next exercise to prepare for having a direct meeting with the person presenting the problem. The best possible time to face this situation is well before it becomes a nightmare. Have a dialogue with anyone affected by your move into a supervisory role. Make it a two-way conversation, emphasizing not only your goals but also your employees' needs and how you might legitimately help meet them.

Remember, even the best dialogue may not solve the problem in a single round. It may take two or three conversations to get the issue resolved.

# Exercise:
## *Passed-over Employee*
## *Nightmare Planning Worksheet*

**Step 1:** Describe the problem with the passed-over employee in behavioral terms. (If necessary, first write it in emotional and judgmental language, and then edit it.)

_____

_____

_____

_____

_____

_____

_____

_____

_____

**Step 2:** Decide how you plan to approach each element of G-R-E-A-T.

_____

_____

_____

_____

_____

_____

_____

_____

_____

**Goals:**

_____

_____

_____

_____

_____

**Roles:**

My Role                          Their Role

_____        _____

_____        _____

_____        _____

**Expectations:**

_____

_____

_____

_____

_____

**Abilities:** "Don't Know, "Can't Do," or "Won't Do"?

☐ **Don't Know:**

_____

_____

_____

☐ **Can't Do:**

- Training: _____

- Changes in the job structure: _____

- Tools and resources: _____

- Reassignment or separation: _____

_How to Cope With Supervisory Nightmares_

☐ **Won't Do:**

- Reasons:

_____

_____

_____

_____

- How you can change rewards/punishments:

_____

_____

_____

_____

**Time:**

_____

_____

_____

_____

_____

_____

## Make an Action Plan

As a result of the dialogue, jot down the steps you will take and that you want the affected employee(s) to take. Steps you might take could be to give these people wider latitude, only review their work when they're finished with a project—not during it (subject, of course, to their maintaining a high-quality work product), have regular private meetings to listen to input and discuss departmental issues, and so forth. When you're willing to change, it makes it far easier for employees to accept change. After setting up the action plan, schedule a follow-up meeting to discuss the efforts you both are making.

You may also wish to try some of the following suggestions to cope with the specific diagnoses made earlier. Integrate them into your communication and action planning.

**Autonomy/independence needs.** If the employee's need for autonomy and independence seems to be the root problem, the issues to consider are, first, whether the employee is fully competent, and second, to what extent he or she can work independently. If you can legitimately give the person the autonomy/independence he or she wants, then you both win: you get the quality of work you need (and fewer negative emotions), and the employee achieves at least some of his or her goals. Notice that the two of you must establish and agree on a certain level of performance and/or quality for this to be successful. If the employee achieves this level, then you can continue to allow him or her to work independently: if not, then you have to supervise more closely.

The following questions can aid this exploration:

- Which parts of the work can be performed independently?

- Which parts of the work can't be performed independently?

- Is the employee able to perform these tasks in a satisfactory manner without supervision?

- If not, can training, tools, or job redesign make the employee better able to work independently?

You may be concerned that empowering one employee to work independently may create a problem with other staff members—and it may. To deal with this issue, first determine ways in which the affected employee is different. For example, he or she may have greater experience, longer tenure, or unique skills, any of which could justify some freedoms not generally available. Such privileges may even serve as an incentive for the other members of your team to develop their skills. If the type of work permits, helping more of your employees to become fully empowered is great! You'll be freed up to spend your days planning and advancing the work, not looking over everyone's shoulder.

**Feelings of being publicly humiliated or having competency challenged.** First, assess the reasons why you have the position and the way in which the promotion situation was handled, honestly and candidly. Does the passed-over employee have good reason to feel humiliated or criticized? Sometimes the senior supervisors or managers who made the decision caused the problem the two of you are dealing with.

Second, make a list of the employee's competencies and talents. Set as a personal goal that you will, to paraphrase Ken Blanchard's famous statement, "catch the employee in the act of doing it right and tell him or her about it." Do this regularly and frequently. If the employee has taken a blow to the ego, salve in the form of honest praise for work well done is the most powerful tool in your supervisory kit.

Third, look at the available work. Can the employee be put in charge of special projects, assume additional responsibilities, or be given team leadership roles? Don't give someone extra responsibility just because he or she feels bad though; it has to be responsibility the person can legitimately handle and legitimately deserves.

**Power/control issues.** Encourage the employee to talk with you about ideas and goals for the department and organization as a whole. Discuss the organizational mission and how the department fits into it. Focus on the employee's good ideas and see how many of them you can legitimately use—giving full credit publicly to the source, of course. By helping to get at least some of his or her goals accomplished, you'll enable the employee to feel more empowered and more accepting of your leadership.

If you do use employees' ideas, don't be surprised when they tell everyone how their ideas made you successful. Smile, agree, and go on with your work. The best way to get the credit is to be unfailingly generous in sharing it.

**Personal competitiveness.** Take this opportunity to be generous in your victory. If it was a good race, the other person also has talent and ability—otherwise, it wouldn't be satisfying to win. Now your challenge is to turn his or her talent and ability to good use for both of you.

Accept that other people do some jobs differently and better than you do. One of the worst offenses you can ever commit as a supervisor is to hire clones of yourself or only people less able than you. In fact, if competitiveness is the issue, take some time to list the jobs the affected person does differently and better than you. By recognizing the superior talents of others, complimenting them, and then assigning them the projects at which they excel, everybody wins: you, by having a more productive department; the other person, by gaining self-esteem and recognition; and the organization, by getting more and better work accomplished.

**Negative attitudes about the organization.** Try to talk with the employee about negative attitudes you perceive, but understand that some people will not and cannot listen to such feedback, and will reject your interference. Ultimately, if this employee's anger and resentment grows great enough, he or she will have to be separated from the organization, even if work performance is otherwise good. As a supervisor, focus on actual behavior (including acting out and public displays of anger and resentment), not on "attitude."

## Decide What to Do If Dialogue Doesn't Work

If no change results from your efforts, you must evaluate your next steps. First, assess the seriousness of the problem. If the passed-over employee clearly doesn't like you, but he or she does the job, doesn't challenge you publicly, and faces you privately only on work-related issues, no problem. Accept that supervisory relationships aren't perfect and move on.

If the employee chooses to fight you, undercut you, refuse to work, or become actively insubordinate, you must act firmly. Confront the behavior and draw lines of acceptable and unacceptable challenges. Acceptable behavior is to tell you privately and professionally that he or she disagrees with your decision; unacceptable behavior is to call you stupid at a staff meeting and walk out of the room. Document incidents of unacceptable behavior. Try informal counseling, and then move into the formal disciplinary process of your organization if necessary. At that stage, keep a close eye on your own attitude and conduct: you have to behave professionally, regardless of the provocation. While not all these situations can be successfully resolved, most can be.

# Help! I Have a Know-It-All Employee

*If he opens his mouth at one more staff meeting, I think I'm going to scream! He's so invested in explaining everything to everybody that he won't shut up for a minute. He does have expertise and knowledge, I admit, but the way he has to shove it in everybody's face makes me want to ignore everything he has to say.*

*She acts like she's being so polite and helpful when she takes me aside, shakes her head, and says in that patronizing tone of hers, "Let me give you a little helpful advice." For every time the advice is on target, there must be ten times when it comes straight in from left field. It has absolutely nothing to do with the real situation. Besides, I'm the boss. Shouldn't I get shown some respect?*

*I've never met a man who can make ignorance sound so authoritative. At first I thought he knew what he was talking about, because he sounds so good. In practice, though, he makes these oratorical pronouncements that turn out to be 100 percent dead wrong. Try to point it out, though, and here comes every sophomoric debating trick in the world. He's not only doing his work correctly, he keeps twisting it around into my fault. Something's got to change—now.*

Know-it-alls and office experts come in two basic flavors: people who really do know a lot, even if they're less than tactful in how they express it, and people who don't know nearly as much as they think or pretend. Both types can easily turn into supervisory nightmares—the real experts for their patronizing tactics that leave resentment in their wake, and the fakes for wasting time, making mistakes, and shifting blame.

The need to always be right, to always have the floor, to always have the last word, usually results from a personal self-esteem issue. This is true for both employees who really do know it all and those who only think they do. A strategy for managing this variety of employee nightmare follows.

## Diagnose the Situation in Behavioral Terms

What is it about the behavior of your know-it-all that is the actual problem— disrupting meetings? keeping others from getting work done? wasting time? Why does he or she behave like this? Let's look at possible scenarios.

**Need for personal validation.** While you may be tempted to scream the next time this person opens his or her mouth, that tendency often only increases the problem. People who talk all the time feel (usually with some justification) that they aren't listened to. This makes them more insistent, which makes others want to listen to them even less, and the cycle of reinforcement persists.

**Inappropriate communications skills.** Some people are tone-deaf to the way they come across. A person who talks incessantly at meetings and continues the debate long after the rest of the group has reached consensus may be genuinely unaware of how the process is supposed to work.

**Need for power and control.** If the know-it-all constantly advises you about your management strategies, the issue may be a need for power and control.

**Insecurity.** Know-it-alls frequently blast away to offset feelings of insecurity or fears of incompetence. Their behavior gets them recognized and thus provides a necessary sense of importance.

**Lack of appropriate motivation.** Remember, people don't behave as you want, but as they are motivated. The know-it-all gets a benefit from the behavior or a punishment from avoiding (the "won't do" issue). How can you change the motivational environment?

## Recognize and Deal With Your Contributions

If you are showing active irritation with the "expert's" behavior, not wanting to credit his or her ideas because of the way they are presented, or getting defensive because you feel constantly patronized, how can you deal with your own emotional issues? Can you provide more legitimate praise and positive feedback to meet this person's needs for appreciation?

## Face the Problem Head On (Communicate!)

Based on your assessment, plan a communications approach and initiate a dialogue. The Negative Feedback model is more appropriate than the GREAT model in this situation. Use the format in the following exercise to prepare for this conversation.

# Exercise:
## Know-It-All Employee
## Nightmare Planning Worksheet

**Step 1:** Describe the problem with the know-it-all employee in behavioral terms. (If necessary, first write it in emotional and judgmental language, then edit it.)

_____

_____

_____

_____

_____

**Step 2:** Tell the person about your concerns, using the Negative Feedback Model.

   1. Define the problem in behavioral terms (use a specific incident or two; don't be general).

     _____

     _____

     _____

     _____

     _____

   2. Relate the impact and your feelings (how it affected you or others; how it affected the work to be done).

     _____

     _____

     _____

     _____

     _____

3. Ask—then *listen!*—for the real problem (what did you hope to achieve? how could we change?).

_____

_____

_____

_____

_____

_____

4. Work out a win/win change (what will you both do?).

_____

_____

_____

_____

_____

5. Focus on the positive elements of the relationship (his or her desire to contribute, the good ideas presented).

_____

_____

_____

_____

_____

## Make a Plan

Focus on steps you're willing to take as well as on those the other person needs to take. You might agree to have regular meetings to listen to his or her input, plus you might accept his or her legitimate expertise in some specific areas and actively seek out suggestions in those areas.

Below are some suggestions for coping with the specific diagnoses offered earlier. Integrate them into your communication and action planning.

**Personal validation issues.** Although it may seem counterproductive, often the very best strategy is to validate these people. Praise their knowledge and insight. If the know-it-all's idea is not going to be accepted, offer the person praise and thanks for contributing it anyway. It was a good idea, a thought-provoking idea, an inspirational suggestion, a valuable counterargument—whatever you can honestly say.

A good phrase to use is, "If I understand you correctly...," especially when you don't want to validate the statement. This feedback approach helps confirm that you understood and heard the employee, even when you may still strongly disagree.

**Inappropriate communications skills.** If this reflects your situation, you must work on the slow process of education. Although you may think it's completely unnecessary, you may in fact have to say, "We've finished with this issue for now, and it's time to move on. If you have additional points, you may submit them in a memo, but for now, we're going to move to the next item on the agenda." The person may in fact not know this. Don't take the behavior as a challenge to your authority; merely point out the true situation in a clear, calm voice.

**Need for power and control.** Again, listening and validation are powerful tools. Accept the know-it-all's good ideas and don't be threatened when he or she takes credit for your success. Smile, agree, thank him or her, and go back to work. Others will quickly figure out the truth.

**Insecurity.** If this is the source of your problem, look for the things the "expert" does well and make sure you single him or her out for praise. Build self-esteem in the areas where this employee merits encouragement, and watch his or her security increase—right alongside work performance.

**Lack of appropriate motivation.** Some people turn into problems because they're not rewarded for their work in a way that meets their needs. Remember, motivation is highly individual; you need to find out what kinds of rewards this particular person seeks. There are three ways to find out someone's personal motivators:

- Ask ("How would you like to be rewarded for your excellent performance?")

- Observe (Under what conditions does the person seem to behave properly?)

- Experiment (Try different approaches and see what works.)

## Decide What to Do If Dialogue Doesn't Work

If no change results from your efforts, think about trying to set ground rules for proper behavior. Negotiate them with the person, remembering that as supervisor, you are allowed to insist on rules even though the employee doesn't necessarily like them. For example, you might set a speaking time limit for meeting participation. If the employee fails to respect the rules and limits you set, assess the overall seriousness of the problem in light of the positive aspects of his or her performance, and then proceed with counseling and the formal disciplinary process.

# Help! People Keep Going Behind My Back

*I thought there was supposed to be something called a chain of command, but as far as one of my staff is concerned, there's no such thing. He's regularly camped out in my boss's office tattling about every little thing that isn't to his liking—but he'll never talk to me about it. Worse, he distorts and exaggerates and sometimes just plain lies. Then my boss calls me in and I'm on the hot seat. When I talk to the employee about it, he says he's just doing his duty to the company. When I talk to my boss about it, she asks me what I'm so afraid of. My position is being eroded daily.*

*I know my boss used to be her direct supervisor, but now I am. They're still friends, though, and they go out to lunch at least every week or so and gossip together. I know I shouldn't be paranoid, but I feel that their relationship is a threat to my authority. If I tell her to do something she doesn't like, she says, "Well, Harry never made me do that." Yeah, but I'm not Harry. If I insist or try to discipline her, I'm afraid I'll be in hot water with my boss.*

*My boss has an "open door" policy, and it seems to me that the primary purpose is to encourage my staff to have a direct relationship with her. She gives work assignments to them without checking with me—and I usually already have work assigned to them—changes my directives without consulting, and generally undercuts me at every turn. I tried talking with her, but she made it clear that she's the boss and she can do whatever she wants.*

If your employees find it easy to go around you directly to your own supervisor about routine departmental matters, you have two problems: one with the employee, the other with your supervisor.

The "chain of command" isn't supposed to place a padlock on your supervisor's door. Most organizations are informal enough that a certain amount of direct contact between your staff and higher levels of management is normal. It may be uncomfortable or awkward, but you have to accept it as a normal part of your operating environment.

This becomes a nightmare situation when it goes beyond the normal give-and-take of an open organization. If your staff takes negative messages about you or your department to your supervisor without ever confronting you, that's a problem. They are certainly entitled to contact higher levels of management if they aren't satisfied with your decisions or your conduct, and to even file grievances if they feel it's necessary. But virtually every organization—at least on paper—insists that employees first try to work out problems with their supervisor.

Another nightmare scenario is the one initiated by your own supervisor. If your boss occasionally goes directly to one of your staff members with a small, immediate job assignment, that's a legitimate use of their supervisory prerogative. Your staff is his or her staff too. If your boss countermands your orders or policies, changes employee priorities, or regularly gives major job assignments to staff members without checking first with you, that's a problem. Such behavior sows confusion among your employees, undercuts your legitimate authority, and interferes with the flow of work. The proper sequence is for your boss to give the assignments to you and for you to pass them on. That allows you to keep control of your work situation.

The same five-point plan detailed in the preceding chapters will help you manage chain-of-command nightmares.

# Diagnose the Situation in Behavioral Terms

In this situation, you must analyze two different sets of conduct: the employee's and your own supervisor's. Depending on the situation, you may need to spend more effort on one than on the other. The first step, though, is to get out your organizational "stethoscope" and diagnose the problem.

**Advancing personal agenda.** If an employee has easy access to higher levels of management, it makes sense that he or she would want to take advantage of it. After all, every book on mentoring and networking emphasizes the value of high-level allies and information sources. As a first-level or second-level supervisor, you have limited power to promote or advance your staff; your boss always has more. So far, this is natural and not necessarily a nightmare scenario.

Some employees take it farther, though, deciding that if you lost your position, they would gain by it. Undercutting you regularly with your own management seems a sensible strategy to pursue—nothing personal, of course. Occasionally the employee harbors a dislike, and uses access to management to sabotage you. That *is* personal, of course.

**Office politics.** You have less power than your boss in an organizational setting. That means, regardless of desire or intent, you can't make certain decisions or offer employees options that your boss might be able to provide. Employees with free access to upper management may decide to cut through the red tape in behalf of organizational issues, personal pet projects, or other goals. You might not have the power to say "yes" even if you want to; your boss is in a different position.

**Lack of awareness of appropriate behavior.** The concept of the chain of command doesn't register with all employees. Some people, either through blindness or a rejection of normal office procedures, simply ignore the protocol or don't recognize that it exists—or applies to them. They blithely wander to see whomever they please, and don't understand why you or anyone else could possibly be upset.

**Insecurity about personal role and authority.** A recently-promoted second-level supervisor may be experiencing some insecurity of his or her own, especially if that person used to run the section you now supervise. Perhaps you've experienced the supervisor who leans over your shoulder to do your job instead of concentrating on his or her own. We have a tendency to take this as a personal reflection on our ability, but it's often just the natural reaction of people insecure with new responsibilities. They know how to do your work, and pushing you aside to do it is a way of making them feel more secure.

**Concern about your management skills.** A supervisor who has difficulty in confronting you may have some concerns about your management skills and not feel comfortable talking with you directly. By going around you and/ or developing his or her own sources of information, the supervisor feels that he or she is dealing with the situation.

It's never a bad idea to actually reassess your management style to see if there are real problems that you could correct or change. Look at areas such as organizational ability, communications style, staff assessment, skill development, and technical ability. Consider asking for feedback from managers and peers both in and outside your own chain of command.

**Lack of awareness of problem.** Sometimes supervisors aren't aware that they're disregarding the chain of command, or how often they're doing it. It may be they don't see the negative consequences—only the positive ones (getting assignments passed out quicker, having more direct control).

## Recognize and Deal With Your Contributions

"Even paranoids have real enemies," the old joke goes. If you're feeling emotionally anxious and threatened, and think people are out to get you, these are normal reactions. The feelings may or may not be the truth, though, or at least not the *whole* truth.

Especially in a new position, when you have some insecurity about your ability or you're having some trouble coping, even the hint that others aren't respecting and supporting your position can be quite upsetting. Keep notes for a few weeks about the number of times and circumstances of people violating the chain of command, in both directions. What are the actual behavioral consequences? Is your authority really being eroded?

If you feel the emotional pressure building and think you may be yielding to a little bit of paranoia about this issue, use the information in Section 1 on coping with the emotional burdens of supervision as a way to calm yourself down. On the other hand, don't ignore a real threat.

## Face the Problem Head On (Communicate!)

Based on your assessment, plan a communications approach and have a dialogue. Use the format in the following exercise to prepare for conversations with your employees and with your supervisor.

Discussing this situation with your supervisor will be more difficult and more emotionally challenging than discussing it with an employee because of the power dynamic. You can give negative feedback successfully to your supervisor if you do it in a calm fashion, emphasizing *organizational* issues, not *personal* ones.

> For example, "You asked me to get the Smith proposal out by Tuesday. When you told Suzie to give you budget figures, she naturally assumed that I knew about the assignment and that it took priority over everything else, and she stopped writing her section of the Smith proposal. This nearly caused us to be late. Of course, you have priorities and issues that we all want to accomplish. Could I ask what your goal was in this process so that we can avoid a potential problem in the future?"

# Exercise:
## *Chain-of-Command*
## *Nightmare Planning Worksheet*

**Step 1:** Describe the problem with the employee and/or the supervisor in behavioral terms. (If necessary, first write it in emotional and judgmental language, and then edit it.)

_____

_____

_____

_____

_____

_____

**Step 2:** Tell the person about your concerns, using the Negative Feedback Model.

_____

_____

_____

_____

_____

1. Define the problem in behavioral terms (use a specific incident or two; don't be general).

_____

_____

_____

_____

2. Relate the impact and your feelings (how it affected you or others; how it affected the work to be done).

_____

_____

_____

_____

_____

3. Ask—then *listen!*—for the real problem (what did you hope to achieve? how could we change?).

_____

_____

_____

_____

_____

4. Work out a win/win change (what will you both do?).

_____

_____

_____

_____

_____

5. Focus on the positive elements of the relationship (respect employees' or supervisor's legitimate interests, value advice given or feedback received, appreciate willingness to accept feedback).

_____

_____

_____

_____

_____

## Make a Plan

Focus on the steps you're willing to take as well as on steps you need the other person to take. You might suggest more regular meetings with your supervisor to coordinate work schedules and priorities. You might work at accepting more direct employee/management contacts, or set broad parameters of acceptability.

In addition, here are some suggestions for coping with the specific diagnoses described earlier. Integrate them into your communication and action planning.

**Advancing a personal agenda/playing office politics.** The first challenge is to uncover the political or organizational agenda and to determine whether it's personal with you. If the employee simply sees relations with higher management as a ticket to career advancement, your goal is to negotiate acceptable limits. You can point out that you have some influence on his or her career prospects. By supporting the employee's agenda, you can negotiate toward a win/win outcome.

If the issue is personal, you have to confront it directly. Listen to the person's gripes, deal with any legitimate ones, and then clearly and firmly set out ground rules involving the chain of command. Enforce them.

If the personal issue involves the employee's relationship with your supervisor and that relationship doesn't involve you, be careful. In one of the scenarios that led into this chapter, the second-level manager and the employee were old colleagues and friends. You won't get anywhere interfering in that relationship, but it's appropriate to discuss where the line should be drawn.

Even more sensitive is the situation where one of your employees is romantically involved with your boss. At this point, you're playing with fire. Do not assume that rational business thought will automatically or necessarily be welcome here. Do discuss the situation with your supervisor—not with the employee—to see if you can work out acceptable ground rules. If the affair is officially secret (no matter how many people know or suspect), act as if no relationship exists—only a friendship.

**Lack of awareness of appropriate behavior.** This is a classic "Don't Know" problem. You need to explain the logic of the chain of command, the consequences to the department of breaking it, and the rules and procedures that exist in your organization concerning the chain of command. It may be difficult for you to accept that an employee is truly oblivious to the right way of doing business, but that may well be the case. To help him or her accept the rules, also explain what sorts of relations and contacts with upper management are acceptable.

If the employee won't accept a reasoned approach, your next step is to lay out clear rules and procedures and insist they be followed.

**Insecurity about personal role and authority.** Your supervisor always wants at least a few basic things from you: getting your section's work done with the least number of problems, advancing his or her career and organizational goals, and supporting his or her work priorities. Insecure people often act out their insecurity; your strategy must be to support your supervisor, build his or her self-esteem, and achieve his or her goals. Only as the supervisor becomes more secure will this problem ease.

**Concern about your management skills.** Ask for feedback from your supervisor about your management of the department or section. If you suspect or know your areas of weakness, ask about them. Show through your listening skills that you want feedback and will react constructively to it. By accepting feedback and making improvements, you gain more ability to give feedback and changes yourself.

**Lack of awareness of problem.** As with any "Don't Know" problem, stating the issue clearly, calmly, behaviorally, and unemotionally is most likely to achieve the goal.

# Decide What to Do If Dialogue Doesn't Work

With an employee, if you have had a dialogue and agreed on steps and then the steps aren't followed, the next step is to lay down the rules. State clearly what you expect and respond directly whenever you don't get it. If you have your boss on your side, you can enlist his or her support by sending the employee back to you.

You'll have some difficulty disciplining or terminating an employee for this problem if management isn't willing to help you. On the other hand, an employee who is causing a problem here will usually be causing other problems too. Focus your attention on these deficiencies in work conduct and behavior in other areas. Document them. As you move on to the formal discipline track, the employee's credibility in the eyes of management will drop, especially if you have documented the deficiencies in behavioral terms.

With your supervisor, all you can do is ask for the behavior you want. If the supervisor refuses, then you have to adapt to his or her wishes, no matter how things are supposed to be. Ask for guidance on conflict issues. For example, if your supervisor goes directly to an employee and changes his or her priorities without telling you, ask what your supervisor expects you to do about the work left unattended.

While asking employees to tattle about management's visits won't work, you can require your staff to tell you about any work assignment they receive that takes more than, say, twenty minutes to complete, or that interferes with an assignment or priority you have given. You can hold them responsible for the work you give them, regardless of other assignments they receive, if they fail to inform you.

# Help! I'm Supervising an Employee Older Than Me

*It's been nonstop resentment ever since I became his supervisor. Every time I tell him to do something—anything at all—he starts in on me. "That's not the way we do things around here." "We tried doing it that way about six years ago, and it was a total disaster." "Don't tell me how to do my job. I've been here longer than you've been alive." Unfortunately for him, part of my job is to change things and to tell him how to do his job differently. How can I get him to accept the need for change and do his job the new way?*

*She's not that much older than I am, but she has been here longer. She has contacts and friends throughout the company, and she's using them to undercut me and make me look bad, but the truth is she's not doing the work. She seems to think that her seniority means she shouldn't have to work as hard as anybody else. "You're the supervisor," she sneered at me the other day. "That's what you get paid to do. All you're trying to do is palm off your responsibilities on me."*

*"I've outlasted ten supervisors," he said. "You come in here with your great ideas, you don't listen to the voice of experience—it almost seems like you think experience is a negative thing—you make grandiose changes, and in the end it all comes back to the same old thing. Don't expect me to get excited. I'll do my job, but don't push me."*

Historically, age and rank tended to go together. You became a supervisor at least in part because you stayed a long time and earned your stripes. Today, in an environment of change and innovation, this is not nearly as often the case. Youth is associated with lower fears of computer technology, more responsiveness to rapid change, less need to retrain—and, let's face it— lower cost.

Some suspicion is natural when a significantly younger or less experienced person begins to supervise older and senior employees. Part is suspicion about you—are you really qualified for the job? Part is suspicion about the organization—is this a prelude to getting rid of the older people altogether?

Compounding this problem are some of your own fears. Will you be accepted or challenged? How do you feel about giving orders to people who might be your parents' age? Are you secure in your own knowledge and ability?

This mutual suspicion can poison a relationship before it starts. However, there is an alternative: resolve to value the knowledge, ability, and strengths of the older person and use that to create a win/win relationship. And if an older/senior employee nightmare develops nonetheless, use the following five-point plan to overcome the problem.

## Diagnose the Situation in Behavioral Terms

If you have this particular supervisory nightmare, the first step is to describe the problem behavior and try to identify the reasons for the conflict. Here are several options:

**Feeling of public humiliation or competency challenge.** An older/senior employee may feel humiliated or embarrassed to be supervised by someone significantly younger or less experienced—it could be considered a reflection on his or her competence, talent, or flexibility. A person who feels humiliated or criticized is predictably going to be angry and resentful and eventually act out.

**Career insecurity.** The older/senior employee may feel that having you placed in charge is a hint from management that he or she is ready to be "put out to pasture." The feeling is common whether or not management really has that intention. These employees may assume they're no longer considered a forward-looking part of the organization, no longer valued for their contribution, and possibly even considered a liability.

**Need to prove their worth.** An older or longtime employee normally does have real competence, skill, and experience to contribute to the organization. Occasionally, though, he or she may perceive more ability than is really the case. By pushing for their preferred way, by going in their own direction regardless of your wishes, by continuing to argue for their ideas, these people are trying to prove their worth to you and to the organization.

**Negative feelings about the organization.** Some employees experience a steady shrinking of morale and positive attitude in the course of their career. They did not receive rewards or advancement over the years; they may not have had their personal or ego needs met. As the classic management cartoon says, "I must be a mushroom. They keep me in the dark, they feed me manure, and then they can me." They have become disenchanted with the organization—they've quit, but stayed. This attitude is revealed in expressions of cynicism about any new idea, program, or activity. "Yeah, right," the employee thinks, and often says.

**Need for autonomy and independence.** After many years on the job and having demonstrated a certain level of ability, the senior/older employee may simply value being left alone to do the job.

## Recognize and Deal With Your Contributions

Your contribution to this sort of nightmare may be significant. When you supervise people who are older, more senior, and more experienced than you are, it's normal to feel insecure or threatened. Entering management ranks always carries a price of personal insecurity; this particular situation only makes it worse. By trying too hard to demonstrate authority and take control, you participate in escalating natural friction into a major nightmare.

In some circumstances, supervisors in this position have their own psychological issues, especially if the problem employee is their parents' age. Because of this, they may fail to exercise legitimate authority, fail to point out less than satisfactory performance, or fail to insist on necessary changes. The balancing act here is to be assertive without becoming overcontrolling.

## Face the Problem Head On (Communicate!)

Based on your assessment, plan a communications approach and initiate a dialogue. Use the format on the next page to prepare for conversations with employees.

# Exercise:
## *Older/Senior Employee*
## *Nightmare Planning Worksheet*

**Step 1:** Describe the problem with the employee in behavioral terms.
(If necessary, first write it in emotional and judgmental language, and then
edit it.)

_____

_____

_____

**Step 2:** Decide how you plan to approach each element of G-R-E-A-T.

_____

_____

_____

**Goals:**

_____

_____

**Roles:**

My Role                                 Their Role

_____          _____

_____          _____

_____          _____

**Expectations:**

_____

_____

_____

**Abilities:** "Don't Know, "Can't Do," or "Won't Do"?

☐ **Don't Know:**

_____

_____

_____

_____

☐ **Can't Do:**

• Training: _____

• Changes in the job structure: _____

• Tools and resources: _____

• Reassignment or separation: _____

☐ **Won't Do:**

• Reasons:

_____

_____

_____

_____

• How you can change rewards/punishments:

_____

_____

_____

_____

**Time:**

_____

_____

_____

# Make a Plan

Focus on the steps you're willing to assume as well as on those you need the other person to take. A win/win agreement with these employees is achievable because they have real contributions to make to you and the department. Ask to set up regular meetings to solicit their input. Review your ideas and direction with them to gain the value of their experience and insight, and make sure you listen to their suggestions carefully, even if you don't end up following them all. Ask them to teach younger and less experienced employees, and offer them opportunities for their own training and development (understanding that they may have fears about learning new areas). Try to negotiate a pledge of noncompetition. Find out what their career goals are and work to help fulfill them.

Helping an older or senior employee get training and develop new skills is particularly powerful. Sometimes employees in this category are overlooked because they lack updated skills, especially in areas involving new technology or new approaches to work.

When you've zeroed in on one or more of the specific diagnoses detailed earlier, the following suggestions will provide assistance in coping with your assessment. Integrate them into both your communication and your action planning.

**Feeling of public humiliation or competency challenge.** First, determine whether the older/senior employee has reason to feel humiliated or criticized. Was your appointment to a supervisory position handled well? Has he or she failed to perform well? Second, make a list of the employee's competencies and talents, and make sure you work at recognizing his or her good work. Praise for work well done is one of the best routes toward an improved working relationship and may make useful feedback on weak areas easier. Review any "Can't Do" areas in the "Abilities" section of your planning worksheet and arrange for training, tools, and development activities. Allow the employee the opportunity to vent anger and frustration.

**Career insecurity.** Again, evaluate the extent to which the fears and insecurities are justified. Is the organization planning to lay off older employees? (Although this is illegal, it's not uncommon.) Some of the previously mentioned strategies, especially praise and developmental opportunities, are the best approach here.

**Need to prove their worth.** Help these employees get the opportunity to prove their worth. Listen to their suggestions and ideas and consider them carefully. When you can accept and use their ideas, be generous with the credit publicly. If possible, assign them to projects that will help them earn recognition within the organization. Recognize that while you have real skills and abilities, so do they, and they may have skills in areas where you don't. Use those skills for your mutual benefit.

**Negative feelings about the organization.** You probably won't have much luck facing this issue directly. "Sure, you feel differently, but you're young and you haven't been here long enough to learn just how rotten it is," the older/ senior employee may say. Instead, a better strategy is one of patience and support. The negative feelings about the organization often result from a sense of having been undervalued for years. You can't change this feeling overnight no matter what you do, but through praising and developmental work, you can give such an employee the opportunity for growth—which will often result in a change of heart about the organization. Remember, however, that there's a limit to what you can do here; people must decide on their own how they'll feel about the company.

**Autonomy/independence needs.** This revisits the same issue examined in the supervisory nightmare dealing with an employee who is passed over for promotion. If the employee's need for autonomy and independence constitutes the root problem, the issues to consider are whether the employee is fully competent and to what extent he or she can work independently. If you have the ability to legitimately give this person what he or she wants, then both you and the employee win: you get the quality of work you need (and fewer negative emotions), and the employee achieves at least some of his or her goals. Ask yourself:

- Which parts of the work can be performed independently?

- Which parts of the work can't be performed independently?

- Is the employee able to perform these tasks in a satisfactory manner without supervision?

- If not, can training, tools, or job redesign make the employee better able to work independently?

The concern you might have about allowing the older/senior employee to work independently is usually less than in the case of the passed-over employee. The person's age and experience serve as a legitimizing reason for the extra independence—as long as he or she does get the job done.

## Decide What to Do If Dialogue Doesn't Work

If no change results from your efforts, you must evaluate your next steps. First, assess the seriousness of the problem. If the older/senior employee clearly doesn't like you, but he or she does the job, doesn't challenge you publicly, and faces you privately only on work-related issues, no problem. Accept that supervisory relationships aren't perfect and move on.

If the employee chooses to act out publicly, you must draw a firm line. Fight your own insecurities and set clear ground rules. Sometimes, you have to show the other person that you are in fact in an authority position and that you are reasonably secure in it. You may be surprised at the respect you'll get. Stay respectful, professional, and assertive—any other behavior will likely make the situation worse.

# Help! Two of My Employees Constantly Fight and Bicker

*I feel more like an elementary school teacher than a supervisor of professional staff right now, and it's all because of two of my team members. One or the other is in my office at least five times a day to complain about the other. Truth is, both of them leave a little to be desired as employees. I'm tired of all the blame shifting and petty whining. In fact, I'm tempted just to fire them both.*

*I should have expected trouble when the first day I was on the job Sally came to me to tell me about all the things that Mary was doing wrong. Those two spend more time and energy figuring out how to put the blame for nonperformance on the other person than it would take just to get it done in the first place. "Did so!" "Did not!" It's just like two children squabbling.*

*Well, at least it's work-related. What they fight about, I mean. It doesn't seem so much to be personal animosity as it is a deep-seated disagreement about the right way to do things. They're both passionate about the work to the point of making problems. I don't want to step in the middle every time to make the final decision, since I'm trying to support the team concept, but I don't seem to be able to get those two to settle their differences any other way.*

Dealing with employee-employee conflict is one of the most common problems supervisors experience, and it doesn't take much for this to turn into a full-fledged nightmare.

Often people in an organization work in close quarters for long periods of time, often under stressful conditions, and not surprisingly friction builds and builds. Many employees spend more time with their co-workers than with their spouses or significant others—without the luxury of having chosen them in the first place!

A certain amount of irritation and friction is unavoidable, and most grown-ups can work out minor problems on their own. Let them. A few problems naturally will come to you for resolution, but you should try pushing the affected parties into negotiating their own solution. (This may help avoid starting a pattern in which all petty problems come to you.) When the friction between two people begins to mount, whether of a personal or professional nature, it's time for you to step in. Conflict can grow into open warfare before you know it.

The critical element in coping with this nightmare is firm, assertive management communication, couched in the familiar five-point plan.

## Diagnose the Situation in Behavioral Terms

Two main questions should guide your inquiry:

1. Is there a pattern of conflict between two specific individuals, a pattern of general conflict spreading throughout an entire department, or simply isolated cases of friction and flare-up?

2. Is the conflict affecting work performance in some visible way? If it's not, let it alone.

If the problem is isolated friction and flare-up, step in when the matter crosses the bounds of professional conduct and assertively tell the people involved to work out their differences on their own, and inform you of their decision.

If you determine it's a pattern of general conflict spreading throughout an entire department, the source may be one or two individuals poisoning the well or it may be anxiety or frustration with the state of the organization. After a major downsizing, for example, the remaining employees experience "survivor's guilt." Anticipating a major downsizing can spark competitive behavior and blame shifting in a perverse game of musical chairs.

Even if the clash involves just a few specific employees, their conflict can spread throughout the department. Therefore, you must resolve the problem at its source. If you don't, you may end up with a department-wide nightmare.

Let's look at causes of employee-employee conflict.

**Personal dislike.** Employees don't choose their work mates; therefore, it's not uncommon for people to end up working with someone they dislike. When the dislike begins to dominate the time spent at work and affect the performance of duties, it becomes a problem.

**Disagreements about work duties.** Employees naturally tend to notice their own work requirements more than those of their co-workers, resulting in the "I do all the work around here and [name] just sits around all day" syndrome. "You're supposed to do the filing" one says. "No, you are—plus, you never answer the phones," comes the reply.

**Disagreements about direction or policy.** It's not a bad thing to disagree about departmental direction or policy issues. In fact, if there is no disagreement, you don't need to have most meetings. Each employee brings his or her intelligence, wisdom, and insight to the job, and positive disagreement is a classic technique to get different issues on the table as a prelude to consensus. If one or more people on your team aren't willing to compromise or negotiate, the result is increasing polarization of views and, inevitably, paralysis.

**Real differences in work performance.** People often perceive they work harder or smarter or better than other employees, and sometimes the perception is right. One employee may be carrying too much of the weight, and this comes out in strong expressions of resentment.

## Recognize and Deal With Your Contributions

Supervisors can make numerous tactical errors in dealing with employee-employee conflict. The problem is that each tactic you use can be successful in some situations and bomb in others. Did you ignore the problem? Perhaps that was a wrong decision. Did you step in and make the call? Perhaps that started a pattern, or left one employee disaffected and convinced that you play favorites.

**Ignoring it.** Ignoring the problem is good when it's random conflict, when the issues are minor, and when employees have the maturity to resolve the problem themselves. It's a mistake if the conflict doesn't die down, if the people involved can't solve it on their own, or if work performance is affected.

**Making the decision.** You're the supervisor, which makes you a decision-maker, and sometimes the conflict is presented to you in terms of a choice. Who's right? Who has to do this job? Who wins the argument? You should make the decision when it's an appropriate management decision, when it involves a policy issue, and/or when it brings the matter to a quick resolution. Don't make the ruling if it doesn't matter or if people need to resolve the issue on their own.

**Separating the employees.** The easy way out may be the best tactic as long as separating the warring parties is possible, doesn't create headaches for other staff, and doesn't lead to a precedent you don't want to encourage.

## Face the Problem Head On (Communicate!)

If you have decided to intervene, plan a communications approach and have a dialogue with both staff members together, at least initially (you may need separate, private discussions later). Use the format of the following worksheet to prepare for this conversation.

# Exercise:
## *Employee-Employee Conflict Nightmare Planning Worksheet*

**Step 1:** Describe the problem with the employees in behavioral terms. (If necessary, first write it in emotional and judgmental language, and then edit it.)

_____

_____

_____

_____

**Step 2:** Tell those involved about your concerns, using the Negative Feedback Model.

_____

_____

_____

_____

1. Define the problem in behavioral terms (use a specific incident or two; don't be general).

   _____

   _____

   _____

   _____

2. Relate the impact and your feelings (how it affected you or others; how it affected the work to be done).

   _____

   _____

   _____

   _____

3. Ask—then *listen!*—for the real problem (what did you hope to achieve? how could we change?).

_____

_____

_____

_____

4. Work out a win/win change (what will you both do?).

_____

_____

_____

_____

5. Focus on the positive elements of the relationship (their desire to contribute, the good ideas they have).

_____

_____

_____

_____

**Step 3:** To assess possible conflict in other areas, use the G-R-E-A-T model with both employees in separate meetings.

**Goals:**

_____

_____

_____

**Roles:**

My Role                                          Their Role

_____            _____

_____            _____

_____            _____

**Expectations:**

_____

_____

_____

**Abilities:** "Don't Know, "Can't Do," or "Won't Do"?

☐ **Don't Know:**

_____

_____

☐ **Can't Do:**

- Training: _____

- Changes in the job structure: _____

- Tools and resources: _____

- Reassignment or separation: _____

☐ **Won't Do**

- Reasons:

_____

_____

_____

- How you can change rewards/punishments:

_____

_____

_____

**Time:**

_____

_____

_____

## Make a Plan

Focus on steps you're willing to take as well as on steps you want the feuding parties to take. Are you willing to make certain decisions on their issues? Can you give them private opportunities to work out their differences? Should you schedule regular meetings with them?

Further, there are specific steps you can take to cope with some of the diagnoses identified earlier in this chapter. Integrate some of the following solutions into your communication and action planning:

**Personal dislike.** You may be able to limit sparring partners' contact with each other by making changes in physical proximity or work assignments, but not to the extent that it puts extra burdens on other employees or compromises the quality of work. This is a situation that calls for direct, assertive statements of supervisory authority. State firmly that while there is no work rule that people need to like one another, certain conduct is unacceptable on the job—public arguments and spats, refusal to perform because "it's (his/her) job," disrupting others' work with complaining, and so forth. You may have to enforce this strongly before employees get the idea that you won't tolerate bad behavior, regardless of personal feelings.

Try discussing with each person the performance benefits of working with the other. How does working together benefit the team? What good can come out of working more effectively together? Using the G-R-E-A-T model to define goals and roles can be useful in this context. If your organization operates with a team concept, emphasize the importance of teamwork. Perhaps send one or both to training situations that promote team-building activities.

**Disagreements about work duties.** It's legitimate for employees to need guidance from their supervisors about work rules and specific duties. In fact, conflicts of this type often arise because the supervisor hasn't been sufficiently clear and specific. Two approaches are possible: either set specific duties and make work assignments, or list the duties and ask the affected employees to make their own choices and notify you.

**Disagreements about direction or policy.** The affected people need to be clear about legitimate versus excessive disagreement. There are always boundaries, and your challenge is to describe them in behavioral language. For example, instead of "Harry and John, you talk too much at meetings," try the following:

> "Harry, John, at the Wednesday staff meeting, there were six people present and the meeting took one hour. During that time, you two argued about the new telephone-answering policy for thirty minutes total. In the future, I need you to express your points of view in no more than five minutes apiece. If that doesn't resolve your issue, then I want each of you to write your arguments in a memo within twenty-four hours. We'll have a follow-up meeting of no more than fifteen minutes on your issue. If you can't achieve a mutually acceptable resolution, then I will make the decision and it won't be subject to further debate."

**Real differences in work performance.** If you have identified that the conflict results from real differences in work performance, then you need to focus on the performance issues in order to deal with the conflict. Plan for a developmental conference with one or both employees (depending on who has the actual performance problem). Apply the "Don't Know"/"Can't Do"/"Won't Do" process. Only by resolving the performance problem can you manage the conflict issue.

## Decide What to Do If Dialogue Doesn't Work

If no change results from your efforts at communication, don't give up. Conflict carries a strong level of emotion, not logic, and a single round of dialogue often won't suffice. Review the outcome of the first round. Look again at behavioral issues. Remember, people hating each other is not a problem—people shouting at each other, refusing to work, and interrupting others are problems.

You should gradually become more direct in subsequent rounds of dialogue. Assertively tell people what the ground rules are for dealing with conflict. Make it clear that you won't accept disruption of the office, failure to complete the work, or continual wasting of your time. Unless there is a clear performance issue with one employee but not the other, hold both employees equally responsible for resolving the conflict, and make it clear that any consequences for failing to resolve the conflict will fall equally on both.

If the employees fail to respect rules and limits that you set, proceed with counseling and the formal disciplinary process.

# Help! I Think One of My Employees Has a Serious Problem

*This is the fifth Friday in a row that he came back from lunch smelling of alcohol. His speech was slurred, his walk was unsteady, and he didn't do any work for the rest of the day. I'm scared to bring it up because I'm afraid I'll get myself into legal trouble, but I can't just let it alone, either. I'm caught between a rock and a hard place.*

*She was always a good worker until about six weeks ago; then it was like she had a complete personality change. She doesn't smile, chat with other people, or get involved in the office life at all any more. She walks around like there's a dark cloud over her head. I tried to talk with her about it, but she let me know that it wasn't any of my business as long as she did the work. Now, though, her work performance is starting to slip. I'm afraid she's suffering from some sort of depression and needs a level of help I can't provide.*

*I keep expecting to turn on the eleven o'clock news and hear that he went on a shooting rampage. Seriously, there's something disturbing about him. He's quiet most of the time, until he explodes in a rage when something goes wrong. He acts like there's a conspiracy against him. He bragged about the new AK-47 assault rifle he bought himself for Christmas. I'm getting afraid to talk to him. I hope I never have to fire him or lay him off—I'd be afraid for my life!*

Having employees who behave in a way that suggests serious psychological problems is a real supervisory nightmare. Major consequences can result from mishandling such a situation, ranging from lawsuits to actual physical danger. Many organizations are hiring consultants to set up Employee Assistance Programs (EAP) for dealing with workers' psychological issues, and recently companies have been developing plans for coping with potential employee violence.

As a front-line supervisor with an employee who may have serious psychological problems, you may feel as if there's nowhere to turn. The Americans With Disabilities Act (ADA) forbids discrimination against employees with disabilities, including those of a psychological nature (this encompasses alcoholism and drug abuse). On the other hand, if we know or reasonably should have known that an employee is impaired because of alcohol or drug use, and that employee operates heavy machinery (including using a car to run a company errand) and someone is hurt, the organization may be liable.

On top of that, we tend to feel helpless when confronting psychological issues in the workplace because we aren't (most of us, anyway) mental health professionals with the training and skill to approach such problems in an effective manner. We also don't want a problem with one employee, no matter how legitimate, to spill over and affect other employees. This is a serious situation—a real nightmare.

The good news is there's definitely a strategy to follow if you suspect you have this nightmare, a special four-point approach specifically designed to deal with these sensitive issues.

## Describe the Situation in Behavioral Terms

Just as with any other work-related problem, start with the behavioral description step. What is it you observe in the employee's behavior that alerts you to the possibility of a psychological issue? Examples might be arriving late smelling of alcohol, showing sudden changes in work performance, or displaying abrupt mood changes. List your observations, along with dates and circumstances.

The biggest mistake you must avoid is trying to label a psychological condition when you don't have the qualifications to do so. You aren't entitled to say that someone is clinically depressed—even if that turns out to be the case. That kind of official diagnosis can be made only by a qualified professional, such as a psychologist or psychiatrist. If you say it anyway, it's possible for you to put yourself and your organization into legal jeopardy.

To assist in the potentially difficult process of articulating your unease or suspicions in behavioral terms, do the following exercise—away from work, on your own time. Convert your fears or "instincts" into descriptions of behavior, and then only use this *behavioral* language in your official dealings with the matter.

# Exercise:
## *Behavioral Language*

Write down your fears or suspicions about the employee.

_____

_____

_____    _____

_____    _____

_____

_____

_____

_____

_____

Now go through your written description looking for judgmental language (language that presupposes you know reasons or motives) and change it to descriptive language (language that describes what you observe behaviorally that suggests there is a problem). Be as specific as you can.

| Judgmental Language | Behavior You Actually Observe |
|---|---|
| 1. _____ | _____ |
| _____ | _____ |
| 2. _____ | _____ |
| _____ | _____ |
| 3. _____ | _____ |
| _____ | _____ |
| 4. _____ | _____ |
| _____ | _____ |

## Seek Qualified Help

While you aren't entitled to diagnose mental illness, you are entitled to suspect it. However, if you suspect a problem, don't begin by confronting the employee about it, no matter how good your intentions. Talk to your human resource department first. The professionals in that department have either the necessary training or the power to get outside help to lead you through the minefield—and make no mistake, this kind of situation is a minefield.

Taking this step doesn't mean that you're tattling on a troubled human being in order to get them fired. The goal here is to help the employee succeed on the job and get any additional help needed to cope, such as participation in the EAP. You can't simply send an employee to the EAP or say he or she has a problem and should go to the EAP. The law—and basic human compassion—requires you to make accommodations for a disabled individual, but does not require the impossible. Termination may be an ultimate option, but it isn't and won't be the first thing you consider.

When you approach your human resource department, describe the employee issue in behavioral terms. Share your suspicions, fears, and concerns, but label them as such. Let them direct your next steps. If you aren't comfortable, ask for more guidance. Rehearse any conversations you're instructed to have with the affected employee; role-play with your human resource professionals if appropriate. Keep notes—in behavioral language (no opinions, judgments, or emotional statements!)—on each step.

Inform your supervisor of the situation immediately after talking with the human resource department, or when they tell you to. Why not first? Your supervisor, like you, probably has not had detailed training in these issues and can give you bad directions without intending to do so.

Stick strictly to the script. Do what you are told to do by the human resource professionals. Try to be supportive and friendly to the affected employee throughout the process.

## Maintain Confidentiality

Do not violate an employee's confidentiality, even—or especially—to co-workers. If these team members—who obviously may observe the same behavior you do—come to you, listen to their concerns, acknowledge that you take them seriously, but do not share the specific steps, diagnoses, or actions that result from your work with the human resource professionals.

This is the right thing to do for many reasons:

- The law protects the confidentiality of personnel records.

- The confidence of your employees in you will decrease if you have a reputation for sharing someone else's secrets. (How can they come to you in the future?)

- Maintaining confidentiality makes it easier for the affected person to make a "comeback" if everyone doesn't know everything.

## Get Backup If Necessary

There are still some organizations that don't yet take seriously the requirements of ADA and related laws, or have no plan of response to a threat of violence from an employee, or have no formal human resources department (or whose HR staff is inexperienced in this area). If you don't get appropriate backup and support within your organization, and you are certain you have described your problem in behavioral terms, you are probably best off—on your own—consulting an attorney or an EAP consulting group specializing in these areas to make sure you and all parties are properly protected. These professionals not only can give you valuable advice, but they also may be able to assist the organization with the immediate problem as well as with similar ones in the future. Very importantly, this strategy also gives the affected employee the best shot at getting the real help that will maximize his or her chances for full recovery.

# How to Cope With Management Nightmares

# What Is a Management Nightmare?

New supervisors often experience their jobs as a series of surprises, one right after another. And in dealing with supervisory nightmares, one thing that turns problems into nightmares is the surprise factor. When you anticipate a problem, you normally find yourself better able to deal with it; when the problem comes out of left field, you're obviously at a disadvantage.

One big surprise for the new supervisor is the extent to which your job involves managing up as opposed to down. You know that the first job of any employee is to satisfy the needs of his or her supervisor, and the first need of your supervisor is for you to run a smooth operation that gets the work accomplished with a minimum of headaches. In fact, at first it's smarter strategy to get control of the existing work rather than to initiate sweeping changes, great ideas, and major improvements.

The second need of your supervisor is to know that you are there to be supportive, not competitive. It's certainly reasonable and expected that you want further advancement in the organization. If your boss feels that your desire for advancement is going to threaten his or her own position, you'll naturally get less support. If your boss feels that you want to make both of you look good, your desire for advancement is in fact mutually beneficial.

The third need of your supervisor is for you to adapt to his or her personality style and approach. What are your boss's values? How does he or she like to communicate? What level of detail does this person prefer? Watch and observe your supervisor for the cues and hints that will help you shape your approach.

Nightmares happen with your boss or higher levels of management if you fail to meet these critical needs. They can also happen for other reasons.

Employees always watch bosses more closely than bosses watch employees. Most employees quickly notice any deficiencies or imperfections in their bosses—and there always are some, because bosses, like other human beings, are by definition less than perfect. The trouble is, your boss's deficiencies can have a big impact on you. Managing imperfect people in positions of authority becomes a critical job skill, because imperfect people are the only kind you'll ever know.

A few bosses fit into the "world-class bad" category, but fortunately they're quite rare. Sometimes your only solution ultimately is to go somewhere else. Most of the time, however, you not only can cope but actually prosper if you learn to accept and work with imperfections and quirks. The key elements in this process are the following:

- Understand the office political environment and other wider issues that impact your boss and the department's work.

- Be assertive—not aggressive, not submissive—in communicating your issues in a positive, solution-oriented way.

- Adapt your style and approach to fit the needs of those in authority over you.

- Develop your own network and resources to make sure you achieve the organization's mission.

The "five-point plan" approach introduced in previous sections is valid even when the people involved in the supervisory nightmare outrank you. However, the difference is that you need to look even more closely at your contributions to the situation and figure out more things you can do in planning for an outcome. This doesn't necessarily mean that you're more at fault—only that you have less direct power and must adapt to the reality of the situation.

The next three chapters will look at some common management nightmares and apply effective techniques for solving (or at least coping with) them.

# Help! My Supervisor Is Into Conflict Avoidance

*Why can't she just come out and say so when she thinks I've made a mistake? I'm not perfect as a supervisor, though I try to do the right thing. Not only won't my boss tell me when she doesn't like a direction or action I'm taking, she won't talk to me after the fact. I hear she's upset or angry through the grapevine, but when I ask, she denies it. However, she talks to her boss and I'm afraid my reputation is suffering. I want to resolve this, but I don't know how.*

*"So, you're getting the silent treatment, huh?" When John said that to me at lunch the other day, I suddenly felt better. I thought it was just me. Whenever I did something that didn't please the boss, he'd clam up. The problem is, I couldn't always figure out what I did that backed him off, or why it backed him off, or what I could do to make it right. I thought he hated me. At least now I know that he treats other people the same way. Still, I wish I knew how to get around this problem. He makes me nervous because I never know what to do.*

*My job involves making decisions and selling them. I do the analysis, prepare my arguments, and then make a presentation to the department head, my second-level manager. She nods, thanks me, and seems to agree with my analysis, so I go to work. Then I hear—through intermediaries— that she's gone off and made the opposite decision and didn't tell me a thing! How can I do my job?*

Conflict management is a tough skill to master, and not all people who reach positions of authority in an organization have become good at it. If you're in conflict, someone may end up unhappy. Emotions fly around, and they can be uncomfortable. Some people won't take "no" for an answer, and argue. Fast talkers make others feel overwhelmed and pushed into giving where they don't want to. For all these reasons, managers may avoid certain situations.

Conflict avoidance is a way to get out from under the emotional pressure for some people. Conflict avoiders nod and say nice, positive things to your face, then make an alternative decision behind your back. They send negative messages through third parties. They don't want to discuss the situation with you, and may even deny what they're doing. They may agree with you and then agree with the next person who comes into the office, even if that person wants the opposite.

Bosses who habitually avoid conflict are trying to avoid the pain associated with it. If you can help minimize or eliminate the pain in the conflict, you can often resolve the situation so that both people benefit. When the conflict avoider is higher in authority, you are the one who must make most of the moves. A strategy for doing so effectively follows.

## Diagnose the Situation in Behavioral Terms

As with other supervisory nightmares, start by describing the situation in behavioral terms. What exactly does your supervisor do (or not do) that leads you to believe he or she is practicing conflict avoidance? Is there a steady pattern, or isolated incidents? Does it happen under certain conditions only (lots of pressure, certain areas of the job but not others)? When you communicate with your supervisor about this issue, you need to have details and facts you can present in an objective, nonthreatening manner.

Why is the person practicing conflict avoidance? What does he or she hope to gain from it? Let's look at some common situations.

**Dislike of strong emotion.** Conflict is often associated with strong emotion, and some people have a deep-seated distaste for strong emotions, especially negative ones. Notice that your own personal conflict style can affect the severity of this reaction.

**Fear of higher authority.** Supervisors are always caught in the middle to a greater or lesser extent, responsible for carrying out decisions they may not agree with and taking the heat from the people who are negatively affected. A manager who is under direct orders from a higher authority and can't change the decision may feel very uncomfortable with your resentment or anger. On top of that, he or she may actually agree with you but can't say so without compromising senior management. Sometimes the safest course of action seems to be avoidance, though in reality it usually only postpones the inevitable.

**Not wanting to be disliked.** "If I say yes to John, Sally will be disappointed and hurt, but if I say yes to Sally, John will be disappointed and hurt." Some managers stew over this normal sort of "push-pull" to extremes. If either situation produces the negative outcome of being disliked, he or she may resort to avoiding the conflict or (worse) telling people different things and hoping they don't sort it out with each other. It works short-term, but never long-term.

**Fear of taking personal responsibility.** Managers who don't give you guidance may be looking for "plausible deniability," allowing them to shift the blame because you didn't, after all, do what they said. (You couldn't—they didn't say anything.) This kind of manager doesn't want the responsibility for decisions, especially those that could backfire. Perhaps besides being insecure in his or her own position, such a boss may also fear conflict at the managerial/office politics level.

**Belief that others dislike being told what to do.** Some managers, themselves highly autonomous, fast-thinking, independent types, don't give much in the way of direction because they take for granted you'd prefer not to get it. They assume you think as quickly and in the same way they do, and they are sometimes angry and disappointed when you fail to live up to this expectation. If this is your situation, you will observe your boss's communication is fast, filled with assumptions, and characterized by impatience.

# Recognize and Deal With Your Contributions

Realize that you are the person with the problem, and you are the one who must take the first steps toward a solution. (That you are contributing to the problem doesn't mean you're necessarily doing anything wrong, however.) Let's see how your behavior can play into your boss's tendencies.

**Emotions.** Watch your own conduct and listen to the way you handle conflict. Are you highly emotional? Do you get mad easily? Do you not suffer fools gladly? If your emotions are strong and easily expressed, and this clearly makes your boss uncomfortable, work at lowering the emotional level.

**Pace.** If you're a fast-paced person with a slow-paced boss, the speed of your approach can produce a negative reaction. Your supervisor may be willing to deal with you much better if you slow down and give him or her some breathing room. If the situation is reversed (slow-paced staff, fast-paced boss), again, you are the one who needs to adjust.

**Compromise.** Are you a good negotiator? When things don't go your way exactly, are you able to work with others' needs and goals to see how much you can end up with? The ability to negotiate and compromise can help you immensely in dealing with a conflict-avoiding boss (or anyone).

**Support.** Are you showing your emotional and behavioral support for your boss clearly and regularly? Have you demonstrated your concern for his or her emotional and career well-being? Are you sending the message that you are a team player—on your boss's side—or the opposite?

Use the next exercise to identify your contributions to the problem and what you might do about them.

# Exercise:
## *My Contributions to the Nightmare*

1. What possible contributions am I making to the problem?

_____

_____

_____

_____

_____

_____

2. What steps could I take to gain more influence over the situation?

_____

_____

_____

_____

_____

_____

3. What emotions am I experiencing because of the situation, and how might they be affecting the other people involved?

_____

_____

_____

_____

_____

_____

## Face the Problem Head On (Communicate!)

You can approach communication either on a case-by-case basis or as an overall challenge. The case-by-case approach takes a specific example and tries to work it out. You'll normally have to use the case-by-case approach several times to build a pattern. The overall approach documents several instances and tries for a general conversation about the problem, working toward a solution that will cover all—or at least most—future situations.

With most supervisors, you'll find the case-by-case strategy works best, but you must consider your supervisor, his or her personal style, and the overall state of your relationship. Whichever style you adopt, however, make sure you're well prepared for the dialogue by completing the following worksheet.

# Exercise:
## *Conflict Avoidance Nightmare Planning Worksheet*

**Step 1:** Describe the nature of the problem in behavioral terms. (If necessary, first write it in emotional and judgmental language, and then edit it.)

_____

_____

_____

_____

_____

**Step 2A (if you are planning a case-by-case approach):** Use the Negative Feedback Model to share your concern with your supervisor.

1. Define the problem in behavioral terms (use a specific incident or two; don't be general).

   _____

   _____

   _____

   _____

   _____

2. Relate the impact and your feelings (how it affected you or others; how it affected the work to be done).

   _____

   _____

   _____

   _____

   _____

3. Ask—then *listen!*—for the real problem (what did you hope to achieve? how could we change?).

_____

_____

_____

_____

_____

4. Work out a win/win change (what will you both do?).

_____

_____

_____

_____

_____

5. Focus on the positive elements of the relationship (recognize the other person's position, his or her desire to do the right thing, your support of each other and the organization).

_____

_____

_____

_____

_____

**Step 2B (to approach an overall dialogue on the problem):** Use the G-R-E-A-T model, emphasizing your positive goals in the relationship and how you think you both can work together for maximum mutual results.

**Goals:**

_____

_____

_____

**Roles:**

My Role                                    Their Role

_____          _____

_____          _____

_____          _____

**Expectations:**

_____

_____

_____

**Abilities:** It's possible you have a "Don't Know" problem or a "Won't Do" problem. ("Can't Do" usually doesn't apply in this situation.)

☐ **Don't Know:**

_____

_____

_____

☐ **Won't Do:**

• Reasons (usually discomfort):

_____

_____

_____

• How you can provide positive results:

_____

_____

_____

**Time:**

_____

_____

## Make a Plan

Focus on the steps you're willing to take as well as on those you need your supervisor to take. Review your responses in step 2 of the worksheet as a model. Further, you can integrate some of the following suggestions (based on the previously described "diagnoses" of the problem) into your communication and action planning:

**Dislike of strong emotion.** If your behavior is strongly emotional, work at limiting your own responses. If people don't want to express strong emotion, they really don't want to talk about *not* expressing it either, which limits the opportunity for dialogue. The only way to show them you won't react strongly is by not doing so. Minimize the cost of the conflict in order to help your boss be more willing to share and/or confront problems with you.

**Fear of higher authority.** When dealing with any situation where your boss must answer to others, you must satisfy that issue in order to achieve your goals. First, you must respect and validate the uncomfortable position your boss is in. Accept that he or she has limits. Work at exploring what he or she *can* do rather than *can't* do. You may not get everything you want, but this approach will help you get as much as possible.

**Not wanting to be disliked.** Provide personal and emotional support to your supervisor when you want to know something uncomfortable or awkward, or when he or she has to make a decision. If your boss has a high need to be liked, then work at building a personal relationship. Recognize him or her as a human being. Recognize his or her unique qualities. Express an interest in his or her personal life. Notice positive qualities and actions and point them out. Reinforce the behavior you want and need.

**Fear of taking personal responsibility.** Go very slowly with a manager who has this orientation, and learn to listen for "hidden" messages. (A statement prefaced with a throwaway remark like "By the way ... ," "Just one more thing ... ," or "Do you have a minute?" is often a tip-off for serious and important information.) Make sure you provide first-rate staff support and demonstrate personal loyalty. If a decision seems to be fraught with danger, ask how you both can reduce the risk—for everyone's sake.

**Belief that others dislike being told what to do.** If you are slow-paced and your boss is fast-paced, organize any questions before your meetings. Once in the meeting, ask your questions quickly and assertively. Further, look for fuzzy language in his or her directions or replies: words such as "coordinate," "handle," and so forth are subject to many interpretations. When you hear one of them, ask, "What exactly do you mean by 'coordinate'?"

Second, request regularly scheduled quick meetings for feedback and clarification, especially if you are on a large project. That way, if there's a misunderstanding, you can get it corrected before too much has been accomplished (or missed). An important tip to improve your success in this area is to give your boss a time limit—"I need no more than five minutes of your time."

Third, ask to clarify your authority. All authority situations in organizations involve defining three levels:

- You decide.

- You decide, but run it past me first.

- Bring it to me and I'll decide.

Your job is to figure out in each case where the limits are—which decisions fit into the first category, the second category, or the third.

This kind of approach often works with a supervisor who has a fast-paced, autonomous style, because it's the sort of model he or she personally likes.

## Decide What to Do If Dialogue Doesn't Work

If you tried the overall approach and it didn't work, next try the case-by-case alternative. If you started with the case-by-case approach, be patient; you're trying to train someone to use a different work style, and it doesn't happen overnight.

Make sure your own work remains at a high level of quality—or as high as you can manage under these circumstances. Continue to show support for your boss at all times, even if your emotions are telling you otherwise. (Trying to undercut your boss is always a losing strategy, no matter what.)

Use your networking skills to make sure your efforts and accomplishments are noticed by others, but always make sure you give credit to your boss for your accomplishments. Others in management may know (or suspect) the truth, but they value expressions of loyalty.

Try to develop mentor relationships with managers outside your own chain of command, especially someone in a position to give you candid advice on what might work with your boss or on what you might be doing to contribute to the problem.

Finally, while everybody thinks about quitting once in a while, don't be too quick to give up in this situation. This is a supervisory nightmare in which you tend naturally to be a contributor. Most people can learn to cope with it and develop an effective, if not ideal, working relationship with this type of boss.

# Help! My Supervisor Micromanages and Nitpicks at Everything I Do

*I've been here five years, I worked my way through the ranks into a supervisory job, I know the customers, and I understand my responsibilities. That's why it drives me crazy to be treated like a five-year-old who can't be trusted to handle the simplest thing right. If he has so little confidence in my decision making, why on earth did he make me a supervisor in the first place?*

*Every report I write, every spreadsheet I create, every purchase order I submit has to go through my manager for approval, no matter how minuscule. She has the authority to check my work; I understand that. But I feel as if I have no authority and no responsibility the way she nitpicks at every detail. Plus, every time she finds the slightest detail out of order, I hear about it for days! My staff has figured out that she's going over everything, so they've started checking with her before they come to me!*

*The first thing he said was, "I'm delegating responsibility for the entire project to you. I want you to take the initiative and run with it. I'm concerned with results." But whenever I try, I get pulled up short. He tells me he just wants to make a little "suggestion," but it isn't a suggestion. If I dare to disregard it, I get flack. If I argue or make a counter-suggestion, he just gets his back up. I don't have any real authority at all.*

The overcontrolling manager is a frequent source of supervisory nightmares. When you enter a supervisory position, you take the job at least in part for the ability to make decisions, exercise authority, and get the work done. A micromanaging boss can end up making you feel as if you have no authority and that you're merely a puppet who must do the bidding of higher authority.

Some friction between a first-level supervisor and higher management over the question of authority range and responsibility is inevitable. First-level supervisors operate under restrictions in even the most liberal circumstances. For example, first-level supervisors normally have some hiring authority, but they usually can't fire an employee without the approval of higher management. First-level supervisors may not be able to sign purchase orders, or may have a limited dollar-value authority. That's normal, appropriate, and part of the circumstances of the job.

Senior managers who hold their authority too closely do so for a reason, and understanding the reason is the first step toward improving your ability to cope with this supervisory nightmare. As with the nightmares presented in preceding chapters, there's a sequential strategy for dealing with this one too.

## Diagnose the Situation in Behavioral Terms

Start by describing the situation in behavioral terms. What exactly does your supervisor do that makes you feel he or she is micromanaging? Is there a persistent pattern, or just isolated incidents? Does it happen under certain conditions only (lots of pressure, certain areas of the job but not others)? When you communicate with your supervisor about this issue, you'll need to have details and facts you can present in an objective, nonthreatening manner.

Why is your boss practicing micromanagement? What does he or she hope to gain from it? Let's look at some common situations.

**Perfectionist behavioral style.** Many perfectionists have a love of detail, of process, of precision, and may feel that others who don't share this orientation are careless, mistake prone, or undependable. Under the stress of a busy organization, perfectionism can lead one to grab tightly onto the reins of control and not allow anything to happen without personally checking and verifying that all the details have been properly handled.

**Lack of trust in you.** The issue is sometimes personal—your manager doesn't trust you. Although your behavior can earn this lack of trust, it can also originate with a suspicious manager. Perhaps yours was burned by one of your predecessors, or perhaps he or she is generally not a trusting person. Obviously, if your manager doesn't trust you in the first place, he or she is likely to oversee your work very carefully indeed.

**Need for power and control.** "I worked hard to get to the place where I can make the decisions. Now I'm here, and I'm going to make them." This sort of micromanager is taking and keeping power deliberately in order to further his or her own vision and control needs.

**Fear of mistakes.** "If you do anything wrong, I get into trouble," this kind of manager thinks. An overcontrolling management style is the best way for him or her to feel that mistakes will be minimized. One problem with such behavior, though, is that it stamps out motivation in others, with the result that they don't care very much any more. Since they don't care, they make more mistakes—which confirms the manager's fear and perpetuates the cycle.

## Recognize and Deal With Your Contributions

Since you are the person with the problem, you are the one who must take the first steps toward a solution. Recognizing that you are contributing to the problem, however, is not saying you're necessarily doing anything wrong. Let's see how your behavior can play into a micromanager's tendencies.

**Power needs.** Often the first tendency when being micromanaged is an urge to fight back, to claim the power for your own and hold on tightly. Resisting oversight, pushing for your own decisions, and struggling against overcontrolling behavior is natural, but it tends to confirm and support the manager's preconceived notions.

Further, do you generally have difficulty in receiving negative feedback well? If that's a problem for you, make it one of your challenges to learn to seek out negative feedback and work on the issues raised by it.

**Style differences.** Perhaps in contrast to your boss's style, your interest in details is much less than your interest in the grand strategy. You have confidence in your ability to make things happen and deal with problems as they arise, so you naturally shrug off the perfectionist's concerns—again, confirming his or her fears.

**Mistakes.** Everybody makes mistakes; however, some managers will find yours threatening, and become overcontrolling and micromanage as a result. Being under constant scrutiny is frustrating, and the natural outcome is a tendency to make more mistakes, perpetuating the cycle. The best thing to do is to see your mistakes first and describe what you've learned from them. If you use your mistakes as a learning tool, you'll find they become much less threatening to you.

Use the next exercise to identify your contributions to your nightmare and what you might do about them.

# Exercise:
## *My Contributions to the Nightmare*

1. What possible contributions am I making to the problem?

_____

_____

_____

_____

_____

2. What steps could I take to gain more influence over the situation?

_____

_____

_____

_____

_____

3. What emotions am I experiencing because of the situation, and how might they be affecting the others involved?

_____

_____

_____

_____

_____

## Face the Problem Head On (Communicate!)

As with other supervisory problems, you can approach communication here either on a case-by-case basis or as an overall issue. The case-by-case approach takes a specific example and tries to work it out. You'll normally have to use the case-by-case approach several times to build a pattern. The overall problem approach leads you to document several instances and shoot for a general conversation about the problem, working toward a solution that will cover all—or at least most—future situations.

With most supervisors, you will find the case-by-case approach works best, but you must consider your supervisor, his or her personal style, and the overall state of your relationship. Whichever style you opt for, make sure you come well prepared for the dialogue by completing the following worksheet.

# Exercise:
## *Micromanagement Nightmare Planning Worksheet*

**Step 1:** Describe the nature of the problem in behavioral terms. (If necessary, first write it in emotional and judgmental language, and then edit it.)

_____

_____

_____

_____

**Step 2A (if you are planning a case-by-case approach):** Use the Negative Feedback Model to share your concerns with your supervisor.

1. Define the problem in behavioral terms (use a specific incident or two; don't be general).

   _____

   _____

   _____

   _____

2. Relate the impact and your feelings (how it affected you or others; how it affected the work to be done).

   _____

   _____

   _____

   _____

3. Ask—then *listen!*—for the real problem (what did you hope to achieve? how could we change?).

_____

_____

_____

_____

4. Work out a win/win change (what will you both do?).

_____

_____

_____

_____

5. Focus on the positive elements of the relationship (recognize your boss's position, his or her desire to do the right thing, your support of each other and the organization).

**Step 2B (to approach an overall dialogue on the problem):** Use the G-R-E-A-T model, emphasizing your positive goals in the relationship and how you think you both can work together for maximum mutual results.

**Goals:**

_____

_____

_____

_____

**Roles:**

My Role                                    Their Role

_____        _____

_____        _____

_____        _____

**Expectations:**

_____

_____

_____

_____

**Abilities:** It's possible you have a "Don't Know" problem or a "Won't Do" problem. ("Can't Do" usually doesn't apply in this situation.)

☐ **Don't Know:**

_____

_____

_____

_____

☐ **Won't Do:**

• Reasons (negative consequences of trust):

_____

_____

_____

_____

• How you can provide positive results:

_____

_____

_____

_____

**Time:**

_____

_____

_____

## Make a Plan

Focus on the steps you're willing to take as well as on those you need your supervisor to take. Review your responses in step 2 of the preceding exercise as a model.

In addition, following are some suggestions for coping with the specific diagnoses made earlier in the process. Integrate them into your communication and action planning.

**Perfectionist behavioral style.** The best way to approach a person whose style you know is perfectionistic is to mimic that style. Perfectionists and process-driven individuals believe that a cavalier attitude toward detail is sure proof you're either careless or hiding something—and they will look until they find it. Check your own preparation on job assignments. Ask for feedback on preliminary steps. Ask if there are other details your manager would like in order to feel more comfortable making the decision. As you demonstrate your respect for details, this manager will tend to relax. You may never have the complete freedom or independence you long for, but you can make real improvements over time.

**Lack of trust in you.** Make it easy for your manager to tell you about any areas in which he or she lacks confidence in you. Look for clues and hints about your past failures. No matter how unfair you think he or she is being, avoid getting defensive at all costs—it just confirms preconceived notions. As you pinpoint areas, try to identify ways you can improve. (If you think your boss is criticizing you unfairly, take the attitude that you can always be better, even if you're already good, and work on growth in those areas.) A key strategy is to ask for the manager's advice and guidance on ways you can improve—in other words, seek out negative feedback. Listen and use the advice, whether or not it seems fair. The manager is telling you what you have to do to earn his or her trust. Like it or not, that must be your goal.

**Need for power and control.** Your best strategy here is to demonstrate to your manager that you support his or her career goals and then work to become an ally. By helping your boss gain more of what he or she wants in the organization, you can often gain more freedom and authority yourself. Be careful: This kind of manager is often politically savvy, self-interested, and strong willed. If you are also strong willed and have personal goals, you may find that conflict is inevitable.

**Fear of mistakes.** Identify the specific mistake areas that most concern your manager, and focus your prevention efforts there. Tell your manager what you plan to do in case of trouble. Ask him or her for advice and tips on better ways to avoid mistakes. Always support the manager's worries, emphasizing your commitment to avoid making mistakes.

## Decide What to Do If Dialogue Doesn't Work

If you tried the overall approach first and it didn't work, move on to the case-by-case strategy. If you started case-by-case, be patient. You're trying to train someone to use a different work style, and this doesn't sink in overnight.

Make sure you maintain your own work at a high level of quality—or as high as you can manage under the difficult circumstances. Continue to always show support for your boss, even if your emotions tell you otherwise. Don't get into a direct fight about authority and control—you will lose, because you don't have the power in this situation. You must negotiate and build trust in easy stages.

If the issue is confidence building, negotiation of authority limits, and support of your supervisor's personality style and needs, you can usually resolve this situation over time. Very occasionally, you may have a manager whose control and power needs are so deeply rooted they are impervious to your approach, in which case you may need to find a different manager.

# Help! My Supervisor Yells, Shouts, and Throws Temper Tantrums

*He called when I was out of the office and said he wanted to see me right away. I was over in Procurement straightening out a problem. As soon as I got back, I went straight to see him. "Where the [blank] were you?" he demanded. "Out goofing off, I suppose. When the [blank] did you plan to do some work around here?" When I tried to tell him, he cut me off, growling, "I don't need any [blank] [blank] excuses. Next time this happens, you're fired." How can I work for a tyrant like that?*

*She's a normal person most of the time, but sometimes something just sets her off and she blows up and starts screaming. It's always something minor, but to hear her, you'd think the whole world was conspiring against her. I mean, she gets totally paranoid! Then, twenty minutes later, she comes around and apologizes. I just don't get it.*

*The way he uses sarcasm and belittlement borders on harassment. His favorite management technique seems to be public humiliation. He loves grinding people into the dust, calling them "incompetent" and "stupid" and "worthless." I'm used to it—sort of—but he does it to my staff and I can't protect them.*

Anybody can get angry, have a bad day, or even lose his or her temper. When a person in authority starts shouting and calling people names, the impact goes beyond the actual temper tantrum—managers have the power to hurt people, whether by firing, poor evaluations, bad recommendations, or lousy work assignments. Whether or not that's the outcome, the staff is left shaking in helpless fear, and work suffers.

It's bad enough when this happens occasionally, but when a senior manager displays an anger-driven coping style, the department and the organization as a whole can be damaged. Worse, the anger is often directed at the person in charge—you. First-level supervisors often bear the brunt of this style, which grinds down their patience, initiative, self-esteem, and, ultimately, job satisfaction.

When major outbursts occur frequently, you're facing a major supervisory nightmare. Even though it may seem hopeless, there are steps you can take to deal with this situation. Let's explore what you can do, applying the familiar five-point plan.

## When It Becomes Harassment

Harassment is behavior that violates the bounds of acceptable office conduct. It can be sexual, it can be gender-based, it can focus on race or ethnicity, or it can target someone just as an individual. No matter what from, harassment is a serious matter—it goes beyond supervisory nightmares. While you do have legal recourse if you are being harassed, the reality is that it's still difficult and dangerous if the organization chooses not to be supportive.

On-the-job harassment is a big topic, and one that extends past the scope of this book. If you feel you are being harassed, you should keep detailed behavioral notes (write them *outside* the office and keep them there) and seek professional counsel specializing in these matters.

# Diagnose the Situation in Behavioral Terms

Start by describing the situation in behavioral terms. (You may want to do this at home, in private.) Describe what was said and done, making sure you turn every judgmental statement into a behavioral description. Describe the circumstances. Do you observe a pattern, or isolated incidents? Do the tantrums or angry outbursts occur under certain conditions only (lots of pressure, certain areas of the job but not others)? You need to understand the situation as completely as possible. If you communicate with your supervisor about this issue (there are several strategy choices that may be appropriate), you'll need details and facts you can present in an objective, nonthreatening manner.

Why does your boss behave this way? What does he or she hope to gain from it? Let's look at some common situations.

**Covering up or reacting to fear.** Explosive reactions that come out of nowhere may be a reaction to fear. Rage has a way of putting other people on the defensive, of generating immediate action and response, of making the angry person seem more confident.

**Need to prove superiority or authority.** Some managers need to reassert to those around them that they are in fact in charge. Belittling others or provoking strong reactions helps confirm (in the mind of the manager) that he or she is the only competent one in the place.

**Need for power and control.** If the anger is provoked by a perceived threat to authority, then a need for power and control may be at work. The manager wants to make it absolutely clear who is in charge, and angry outbursts generally make employees jump to attention.

**Style under stress.** The manager who's impatient with anything but results can, under stress, turn into a dictator. Someone who feels everyone else is moving slowly, dealing with side issues, and not cutting to the heart of the issue uses frustration and anger as a motivational tool to speed people up. Sometimes, they're not even aware of their emotional impact.

# Recognize and Deal With Your Contributions

In this, as with many problems you'll have with your boss, you're the one who must take the first steps toward a solution. Remember that although you're contributing to the problem, you aren't necessarily doing anything wrong. Let's examine how your behavior can play into this manager's angry tendencies.

**Power needs.** Your manager may have power needs, but so may you. Getting into a direct power fight with a senior supervisor is a bad idea because you automatically have a disadvantage. You will most likely lose. If you should win, you will have made an enemy for life—and so you lose again.

**Sensitivity.** No one likes to be yelled at, bullied, or mistreated, but some people are more sensitive in this area than others. If you are very sensitive to expressions of anger or disapproval, you may overreact to real incidents or sometimes see minor, normal expressions of irritation in your manager as personal attacks.

**Passive resistance.** Under the constant barrage of attacks, you may have chosen to give up. "Hey, if you have to win and be right, fine!" You acquiesce on the surface, but underneath the fires are still smoldering. You may use the grapevine to vent your emotions and subtly undercut your manager, follow your orders to the letter even though you know they will lead to bad results, and otherwise act out your resentment behind the scenes.

Use the following exercise to highlight your possible contributions to the problem and what you might do about them.

# Exercise:
## *My Contributions to the Nightmare*

1. What possible contributions am I making to the problem?

_____

_____

_____

_____

_____

_____

2. What steps could I take to gain more influence over the situation?

_____

_____

_____

_____

_____

_____

3. What emotions am I experiencing because of the situation, and how might they be affecting the others involved?

_____

_____

_____

_____

_____

_____

# Face the Problem Head On (Communicate!)

You can approach this communication challenge either on a case-by-case basis or as an overall strategy. Case-by-case takes a specific example and tries to work it out. (You'll normally have to use the case-by-case approach, several times to build a pattern.) With the overall approach, you'll document several instances and attempt a general conversation about the problem, working toward a solution that will cover all—or at least most—future situations.

With most supervisors, the case-by-case approach will work best, but you must consider your own situation, your boss's personal style, and the overall state of your relationship. Whichever course you take, make sure you're well prepared for the dialogue (the following worksheet will help).

# Exercise:
## *Angry Manager Nightmare Planning Worksheet*

**Step 1:** Describe the nature of the problem in behavioral terms. (If necessary, first write it in emotional and judgmental language, and then edit it.)

_____

_____

_____

_____

_____

**Step 2A (if you are planning a case-by-case approach):** Use the Negative Feedback Model to share your concerns with your supervisor.

1. Define the problem in behavioral terms (use a specific incident or two; don't be general).

   _____

   _____

   _____

2. Relate the impact and your feelings (how it affected you or others; how it affected the work to be done).

   _____

   _____

   _____

3. Ask—then *listen!*—for the real problem (what did you hope to achieve? how could we change?).

   _____

   _____

   _____

4. Work out a win/win change (what will you both do?).

_____

_____

_____

5. Focus on the positive elements of the relationship (recognize your manager's position, his or her desire to do the right thing, your support of each other and the organization).

_____

_____

_____

**Step 2B (to approach an overall dialogue on the problem):** Use the G-R-E-A-T model, emphasizing your positive goals in the relationship and how you think you both can work together for maximum mutual results.

**Goals:**

_____

_____

_____

**Roles:**

My Role                                    Their Role

_____          _____

_____          _____

_____          _____

**Expectations:**

_____

_____

_____

**Abilities:** It's possible you have a "Don't Know" problem or a "Won't Do" problem. ("Can't Do" usually doesn't apply in this situation.)

☐ **Don't Know:**

_____

_____

_____

_____

☐ **Won't Do:**

- Reasons (payoffs for angry behavior):

_____

_____

_____

_____

- How you can provide positive results:

_____

_____

_____

_____

**Time:**

_____

_____

_____

_____

## Make a Plan

Focus on the steps you're willing to take as well as on those you need your manager to take. Review your responses in step 2 of the preceding worksheet as a model.

In addition, consider the following suggestions to cope with some of the specific diagnoses described earlier. Integrate them into your communication and action planning.

**Covering up or reacting to fear.** If a manager is reacting to a specific incident that poses some sort of threat (such as a report not completed on time), you need to first let him or her vent; second, work on not looking cowed or upset; third, state the specific steps you'll take to correct the situation; and fourth, follow up to show that you have taken the corrective action. Observe this manager to see if certain things set him or her off, and avoid those situations as much as possible.

**Need to prove superiority or authority and need for power and control.** The answer to aggressive behavior is neither to be aggressive in return nor to submit meekly to the abuse. The answer is to be *assertive*. Assertive behavior includes the following:

- Control of your own emotional reactions

- Acknowledgment of the other person's position, needs, and interests

- Firm, clear statements of your own position, needs, and interests

- A commitment to win/win negotiation

If you have trouble dealing with angry reactions from other people, take an assertiveness workshop and practice your skills. Look around to see if any other employees have developed a successful coping style for this manager. You'll normally discover someone who is assertive yet respectful, obedient but not afraid. You can do it too.

**Style under stress.** In addition to standing up assertively to tantrums and other outbursts that your manager falls prey to under stress, make sure that your goal is to do the work well and to be an appropriate and supportive employee. A key tip is that these people tend to regard strong emotional reactions as signs of weakness or as threats—a clear and nonemotional response is best.

# Decide What to Do If Dialogue Doesn't Work

If you've tried the overall approach and it didn't work, try the case-by-case approach. If you started case-by-case, be patient. You're trying to train someone to use a different work style, and the change won't happen overnight.

Keep your own work at a high level of quality—or as high as you can manage under the circumstances. Continue to show support for your boss at all times, even if your emotions pull you the other way.

Don't get into a direct fight about authority and control—you will lose, because you don't have the power in this situation. You must negotiate and build trust in easy stages.

Very occasionally, you may have a manager whose control and power needs are so deeply rooted they are impervious to your approach, in which case you may need to find a different work situation. However, you may discover what others with this kind of manager have already learned: If you deal assertively with the emotional expressions and you earn his or her respect, you'll find yourself with a surprisingly strong working relationship.

# How to Cope With Worklife Nightmares

# What Is a Worklife Nightmare?

There's managing down (your employees), managing up (your managers), and managing sideways—the part of your supervisory role that includes working with other departments, working with the informal organization, working within office politics, working with other supervisors, working with very high levels of management in the organization, working with customers and clients, and in general managing the interface between your department and the rest of the world.

Worklife nightmares result when some part of those essential elements turns bad. If you're a typical supervisor, you can't possibly accomplish your job each day without the willing and voluntary cooperation of others over whom you have no control or authority whatsoever.

There are seven commandments you need to know to cope with worklife nightmares:

1. **Understand the organizational vision and values.** Some organizations have formal mission and value statements, which can help you. (Make sure that your organization takes them seriously before you do.) No matter what your own preferences, your job as a supervisor is always to use your people and resources to advance the organization's mission.

2. **Expand your understanding of people dynamics.** It's essential that you understand where different people are coming from and how you can adapt your style to work with them. The "informal" organization simply accepts the fact that people don't check their humanity at the door when they punch in on the time clock. A supervisor's job is a people job. To develop your skills, study communications, networking, and interacting with people. Build good relationships with everybody possible.

3. **Learn about office politics and the dynamics of power in the organization.** Mao Zedong said, "Power flows from the barrel of a gun," but offices are much more subtle. Power comes from position and job title, but it also comes from respect, networking, persuasive skills, and personal relationships at all levels.

4. **Determine the reach of your own power and influence, and resolve to expand it ethically to the extent possible.** You begin with a certain amount of power for being a supervisor and you add to it by getting the job done, building winning work relationships, demonstrating your trustworthiness, and earning the respect of key people.

5. **Learn the limits of what you can do and what you can't, and narrow your focus to the things you can accomplish.** It does no good to fret about things completely outside your authority and responsibility. The familiar appeal for "the strength to change what can be changed, the serenity to accept what cannot be changed, and the wisdom to know the difference" forms the basis of a good philosophy for supervisors.

6. **Apply the "five-point plan" approach to your problems, from behavioral diagnosis through planning and option building.** Planning is always a powerful tool to get the job done.

7. **Work on your own emotional health, stress management, and personal coping mechanisms.** Review the material in Section 1 and integrate the ideas that fit into your own life.

Now let's look at some common worklife nightmares and how to apply effective techniques to solving (or at least coping with) them.

# Help! Other Departments Won't Cooperate With Me

*Those people in Purchasing act like they're the only people in this company who are busy. You go to them for a simple $25 purchase order, and they look like you've asked them to climb Mount Everest. "We'll try to get to it in the next two weeks," they whine, knowing full well I need it tomorrow.*

*I didn't think I was getting in anybody's way. We needed a new laptop for our on-site travel, and I'm entitled to sign purchase orders for up to $1,500. I found a nice laptop with everything we needed through a mail-order catalog for $1,299, so I placed the order, all inside the rules. Then somebody in the MIS department found out about it and the head of MIS went storming into the vice president's office to complain that I was trying to make an end run around his department. I got called on the carpet, when all I was trying to do was save money.*

*There's this clerk in the supply room whom we all live in fear of. She won't give out a ballpoint pen without six forms and eight signatures. She moves as slow as Christmas and makes you feel like you're killing her. Try to speed her up, and all of a sudden you find that every single thing you need is out of stock. She's a tyrant.*

Virtually all supervisors quickly discover that they can't get their jobs done without the willing and voluntary cooperation of people in other departments—people over whom you have no control or authority whatsoever. Few areas of your responsibility exert as much impact on your overall success as a supervisor than your ability to deal with other departments and to work the bureaucracy like a pro.

In many organizations, departments are referred to either as "support" or "line." A *line* department is one whose work directly results in the product or service offered by the organization. Manufacturing is a line department, as are research and development, sales and marketing, and design. A *support* department (also called "staff," a term of military origin) doesn't directly create the product or service offered by the organization; instead, it offers products or services to the line departments. Personnel is a support department because it offers services to the line departments, not to the customers directly. Accounting (but not necessarily finance), purchasing, shipping and receiving, and building maintenance are also support departments.

Although line departments can certainly be unresponsive, the traditional source of this supervisory nightmare is the conflict between "line" and "support" departments. Line departments in many organizations regard themselves as superior, more important than the support activities. When this attitude prevails in line departments, support departments naturally become resentful, feeling (with justification) that without them the line departments would be unable to function, and that therefore they are as critical to the organization as anybody else—and they're right.

In this situation, conflict can get out of hand and turn into a *bona fide* supervisory nightmare. Instead of line and support working together to meet the organization's goals and serve the customers' needs, the two branches act as if the other is the enemy. As a supervisor coming into an established environment of ill will, there's a limited amount you can do to change the situation. Your best hope is to minimize the conflict.

Even in organizations not torn apart by internal warfare between support and line, you'll commonly see some normal friction with other departments. Everyone is busy, everyone has responsibilities and demands, everyone's resources are carefully monitored (especially in today's competitive business environment), and inevitably some conflict results. This need not be fatal, but you must be aware of the potential for conflict and act correctly. Sometimes normal friction evolves into a supervisory nightmare, when because of personalities, political power games, or some other reasons a support department (or an individual in a department) decides to throw a monkey wrench into your work.

There are powerful strategies you can use—first, to keep the supervisory nightmare from happening, and second, to turn the nightmare situation around.

## Diagnose the Situation in Behavioral Terms

As with other supervisory nightmares, start by describing the situation in behavioral terms. What exactly does the other department do (or not do) that leads you to believe they aren't cooperative? Do you see a pattern, or isolated incidents? Does the problem occur under certain conditions only (lots of pressure, certain areas of the job but not others)? When you select your strategy, you need to be armed with details and facts.

If you're a line supervisor having troubles with support departments, look at the situation from the staff point of view. If you're a support supervisor experiencing conflict with a line department, consider their situation. Why aren't they cooperating? What do they hope to gain from it? Let's look at some common reasons for this nightmare.

**Work pressures.** "Everything's always number one priority around here!" goes the cry. Support departments are often pressured by line departments to make exceptions to policy and switch around work based on the needs of customers and changing situations. In a dynamic organization with lots of work and conflicting customer demands, work pressures can mount and normal friction can evolve into a supervisory nightmare.

Line departments are also under pressure, and their successes and failures are more immediately obvious than those in support departments. This can result in short tempers and a lack of cooperation.

**Exploited by other supervisors.** Support departments in most organizations quickly learn that the claim by a line department that "the contract is at stake!" is not always true. A common practice is to artificially advance your deadlines—called "sandbagging." Both line and support departments can engage in sandbagging. After a while, they begin to look at you as "guilty until proven innocent of trying to sandbag them." Although you may well have a legitimate emergency, the support department has been abused in the past. In this situation, you sometimes will see a particular saying appear on the cubicles of clerks in the support department: "A failure to plan on your part does not constitute an emergency on my part."

A line department not cooperating may feel that its priorities and work schedules are constantly being jerked around by others. Everybody has a claim of immediate emergency, dollars at stake, and personal involvement of powerful executives.

**Need for power and control.** Individuals and departments in some organizations jockey for power and control in the age-old struggle of office politics. One source of real control is the power to delay your paperwork, and this power, used for ill by a support department, can create a classic supervisory nightmare. Line departments may use their supposed superiority and greater importance, access to senior executives (most of whom normally come from line management positions), and customer focus as a way to throw their weight around.

**Negative attitudes about the organization.** If the support department area has lots of cartoons and office sayings posted on the wall (e.g., the laughing workers with the caption, "You want it when?"), read them. Chuckle appreciatively, but realize that these sayings are funny precisely because they articulate real frustrations and real pain. A support department can easily decide that their contributions and hard work are not valued by the rest of the organization. This naturally leads to a negative attitude about the organization itself.

Line departments can also give up under too much pressure or too many projects or insufficient resources or poor leadership. In some organizations where support departments have a lot of power, line departments can feel unable to produce quality work, and this frustration and sense of helplessness leads to negative attitudes (as any reader of the comic strip *Dilbert* knows).

# Recognize and Deal With Your Contributions

With this as in other nightmare situations, when you are the person with the problem, you are the one who must take the first steps toward a solution. And as with other problem issues, the fact that you're contributing to the trouble doesn't mean you're necessarily doing anything wrong.

The primary contribution most people make to this situation is the very natural tendency to regard the problems and issues of their own department as the most important, and not to see clearly the issues faced by the other department. "I really have to have this Tuesday or we'll lose the Smith account," however true, is a statement that focuses exclusively on your pressures and fails to recognize any other issues that may exist.

Another common strategic error is whining and pleading for the other department to do what is, after all, its job—to support you. Whining and pleading are weak, irritating, and, once again, focused on your issues to the exclusion of theirs.

Anyone who's experienced a pattern of noncooperation in the past may walk into the situation with a chip on his or her shoulder. This results in such behavior as dropping the name of a senior executive who wants the job done, going over the head of the clerk who normally handles the work, and other overt or covert threats.

Even just an air of frustration and/or a frayed tone of voice communicates volumes. You can contribute to the nightmare without even being aware of it by the body language you present during interdepartmental interactions.

Use the following exercise to list your possible contributions and what you might do about them.

# Exercise:
## My Contributions to the Nightmare

1. What possible contributions am I making to the problem?

_____

_____

_____

_____

_____

_____

2. What steps could I take to gain more influence over the situation?

_____

_____

_____

_____

_____

_____

3. What emotions am I experiencing because of the situation, and how might they be affecting the others involved?

_____

_____

_____

_____

_____

_____

# Face the Problem Head On (Communicate!)

When you work with nightmare employees, you have authority on your side. When you work with nightmare managers, you're still involved in a one-on-one relationship in your own chain of command. Here, however, you're working outside that chain of command and mostly in a situation that isn't one-on-one. Your issue is most likely with a department, not an individual, and you need a specially tailored communications approach.

The biggest advantage you have in this situation is that the other department usually has a responsibility to do certain things for you, especially if it's a support division. Support staff, after all, make their living providing services to other departments. If your situation is with a line department, normally it also has a responsibility to provide some services to you. The research and development department, for example, must give specifications to the manufacturing department or the product won't be manufactured.

Departmental relationships and how to improve them are a big element of Total Quality Management (TQM). Most TQM programs include the "internal customer" concept, which reflects the idea that departments in an organization provide products and services to one another as part of the overall effort to provide products and services to the "outside customer," who ultimately pays the bills that keep everyone employed.

Here the "internal customer" concept should help you (and the others involved) understand that the way to get departments to cooperate is to treat each other like customers. The customer/supplier relationship is a win/win relationship. The customer wants a product or service and has money; the supplier wants money and has a product or service. Everyone's needs are met. The supplier has to deliver quality, which includes how the customer is treated. To meet the customer's needs requires two critical steps:

- **Find out what those needs are.** You have to ask the customer what he or she wants and needs, why the need exists (so you can figure out how best to meet it), and when and how the needs must be met.

In this supervisory nightmare, the first communications strategy is to find out everything you can about the needs and goals of the other department. For example, let's say the accounting department prints checks every Wednesday, and they need one day's notice to get a new check into the batch for printing. Emergency check requests on Thursday are extremely disruptive. If you don't know how their system works, you may easily create a problem for them—and for you. How do you learn this? Ask. Make an appointment with the department head. Explain that you think you've been causing unnecessary stress on occasion because you don't know as much about their system as you'd like. Explain that you want to know how to work with them in the best possible way. Listen and take notes. Demonstrate your understanding by using the information you learn next time you make a request or send through an assignment. When you demonstrate your willingness to work with their system, you will see improvement (though perhaps slowly) in their willingness to work with you.

- **Recognize them as people.** Courses in customer service always emphasize attitude as well as action. Of course you want to help a customer get what he or she needs. But how you treat the customer and how you show a positive desire have a tremendous impact on how the customer feels at the end of the process. "You get more flies with honey than with vinegar," the old saying goes.

  This does not mean that the way to get support from other departments is schmoozing. Rather, recognize workers as people by polite courtesy—say "please" and "thank you." Learn the names of the individuals in the department and use them. Send thank-you notes to people who go above and beyond the call of duty, as well as a copy to their supervisor and the personnel department.

The next exercise can help you map out some of these strategies.

# Exercise:
## Communications Strategy for Other Departments

1. Ways I can learn about their systems and procedures. What is the best way to meet their needs? What timing and systems issues are most important to them?

_____

_____

_____

_____

_____

_____

_____

_____

2. Who are the people in the department? What are their names and duties? What key personal details should I remember?

_____

_____

_____

_____

_____

_____

_____

_____

## Make a Plan

When negotiating specific projects or actions with the other department, work on creating a mutually beneficial agreement—a win/win situation. "What can I do for you that will make it easier for you to meet my needs?" is the core question. Focus on steps you are willing to take as well as on the steps you need from them. And try some of the following too:

- **Build relationships with the individuals who do the work in addition to the supervisor.** Make sure this is acceptable to the supervisor; don't give the impression of trying to get around him or her.

- **Support their needs and issues.** For example, if a job really isn't top priority, don't pretend it is. Show that you planned far enough in advance so as not to make them suffer. If you are flexible on time or other issues, let them have the benefit of that flexibility. Look for ways you can help them get their work done more quickly and easily. Try to turn over some projects ahead of time and let them know they have extra time before the ultimate deadline.

- **Don't always lean on the same person.** Sometimes one person in the other department has a reputation for cooperation. That person gets overburdened quickly, and the result is burnout. Ask others for help—especially on less time-sensitive work.

In addition, to address some of the specific diagnoses described earlier, the following suggestions may help:

**Work pressures.** If the key issue is work pressure, talk to the head of the other department as far in advance of your needs as possible. Emphasize that your goal is to do as much as possible to make it easier on them, even if it means some extra work on your part. Suggest designating one person as liaison; perhaps the other department can do the same. Treat their liaison as a team member—invite him or her to strategy and planning sessions where the extra expertise may be of help (particularly regarding any part of the project that involves the other department). If you have a party to celebrate the success of the project, invite your liaison (and possibly the department head). After all, they're part of your team.

**Exploited by other supervisors.** The only cure for this is time. If your attempt to be supportive to the other department is rebuffed, it may be because of long distrust and rivalry. Keep with your strategy, but be patient. You have to earn their trust, starting from the "guilty until proven innocent" position.

**Need for power and control.** Be respectful, but assertive. Remember, the other department has a responsibility to meet some of your needs, and the long-range power goals of the department head can't be met if the department gains too difficult a reputation. Be prepared to negotiate for the issues you need. Compromise, adjust your needs to accommodate the other department, use any flexibility you have—but do insist on the basics. Do your homework and know what you're entitled to. Follow up regularly. You must be perceived as strong, but not a rival, and the best strategy for that is assertiveness.

**Negative attitudes about the organization.** You may not be able to change their attitudes about the organization, but you can change their attitudes about you. Follow the basic strategy, emphasizing the validation of people as people. Others will often do favors for you as a person that they won't do for you in your role as department head.

## Decide What to Do If Dialogue Doesn't Work

First, be patient with the approach recommended in this chapter. If your situation has turned into a supervisory nightmare, a substantial amount of distrust and hostility likely already exists. Much of it has to do with wider organizational (and sometimes personal) issues, and may have little or nothing to do with you as an individual. You may be able to change the situation, but it takes time.

Second, be prepared to seek higher authority if necessary to get your critical needs met. You want to avoid this until you've tried the other steps. (For one thing, they won't forget it. For another, your manager may perceive you as weak if you call for help prematurely.)

# Help! The Rumor Mill Is Completely Out of Control

*Ever since XYZ Industries went through their big downsizing, everybody in our company is understandably fearful—if it could happen to our big competitor, maybe it could happen to us. The trouble is, every little rumor gets blown totally out of proportion and each day people are spending hours spreading one story after another. Now I have to spend hours tracking down each rumor and trying to lay fears to rest. Since I'm one of "them"—management, that is—I wonder if I have any credibility here. People seem to prefer believing rumors to believing facts.*

*Are we a company or a talk show? Yes, I've heard the rumor about the supposed affair between two of our department heads, and the one about the couple caught in their car over lunch hour one day. People have personal lives in every company, and I suppose it's natural for co-workers to want to talk about them, but enough is enough! I once had a staff meeting get off track talking about personal rumors, and I had to put a stop to it; now I'm regarded as some kind of spoilsport.*

*I'm convinced that one of my employees is deliberately spreading hurtful rumors about a co-worker, but I can't prove it. It all comes from a personal conflict between those two, but this steps over the line. If I could prove it, I could make it stop, but when I asked the person if she was the source of the rumors, she denied it and threatened to file a grievance against me for false accusations. Now what?*

Supervisors are frequently surprised at the amount of time it takes to manage the unofficial organization, and the rumor mill is one of its major elements. As you've no doubt noticed, rumors also come in many flavors: news leaks about management plans, expressions of fear and suspicion, speculations about co-workers' personal lives, poison arrows of malice and revenge, and so on.

You can't safely ignore the rumor mill for many reasons:

- People act on what they believe to be true, whether or not it is true. If employees in your department are convinced they're going to be laid off, they'll behave as if they're going to be laid off, with all the attendant productivity issues.

- Some rumors turn out to be true. Perhaps a secretary of someone in senior management talked out of turn; perhaps someone in management with an axe to grind has leaked important information. If you aren't plugged into the rumor mill, you may miss information critical to your career success.

- The rumor mill is an important barometer of employee mood and direction. If you know how to listen to it, you can get valuable information.

- You have to be able to act when destructive rumors get out of hand, and you can't act if you don't know about the problem.

- If you appear to be in the dark with respect to the unofficial organization, you may lose influence and respect with your staff.

On the other hand, you can't be seen as too involved with the rumor mill. There's an appropriate strategy for being keyed in without appearing inappropriate, and mastering this skill will help you get past this supervisory nightmare.

# Diagnose the Situation in Behavioral Terms

The first element in this strategy entails how to listen to rumors in a way appropriate to your supervisory role. If you have been promoted to supervisory rank from a staff position in the same organization, you'll normally hear the same sorts of rumors you always have, and perhaps from the same people. If you're new to the organization, you'll probably notice a few employees will bring you some gossip or rumors.

The two mistakes you can make are to be overeager and to be critical of the person who brings you the rumor. Being too eager to hear the latest gossip diminishes you in the eyes of those you supervise. You lose the valuable sense of authority. On the other hand, being critical of people who bring you rumors, being dismissive of them, or cutting them off will result in no more information.

The rumors you encounter will probably cluster in one of the following areas:

**Job-related.** Job-related rumors focus on the company—potential layoffs, changes in strategy, gain or loss of a major client, and so forth. These rumors are either true, false, or have both true and false elements in them. It's not inappropriate for employees to have an interest in such rumors, though it can be dangerous if the stories (whether true or false) suggest the company is in trouble.

A manager of a savings and loan in Wisconsin once wanted to throw a surprise party for a staff member who had been promoted to headquarters. He sent out a memo that read simply, "Staff will assemble for a special meeting Friday at 4:00 p.m." Within half an hour, one of his senior staff came into his office, waving the memo. "What's this all about?" the staff member said, obviously agitated.

"It's just a surprise party for Sally," the manager replied.

The staff member stopped dead. "You've got a serious problem on your hands. Everybody's convinced that our S&L is being closed down and the meeting is to announce layoffs. People are calling their friends, and now there's a huge line of customers wanting to withdraw their money."

Be very careful about job-related rumors. In a nervous business climate, even well-intentioned communication can mushroom into a supervisory nightmare very quickly.

**Personal.** Personal gossip isn't appropriate, but you can't stop it completely no matter what you do. Your attitude toward that sort of gossip—eagerly awaiting each new installment or acting above it all—will directly influence how your staff deals with it.

**Hostile.** One common supervisory nightmare is to learn that someone in your department is spreading hostile or harmful rumors about someone else. This is a serious issue, because malicious rumors can cause a lot of damage. You need to act aggressively and firmly when you disc⊂ ⊃r this taking place. Find out the source and put a stop to it.

## Recognize and Deal With Your Contributions

Two possible areas in which you might contribute to the problem have already been discussed: being overeager and being too negative. You can also contribute to the problem if you've been (or currently are) an active gossip. Spreading stories and passing rumors along is an inappropriate behavior for supervisors and managers. You need to avoid contributing to the pipeline.

Another potential contribution from you is accidentally starting rumors. One of the many challenges of leadership is discovering that idle remarks once ignored now come under detailed scrutiny by those you supervise. "I can't believe how bad sales were last quarter," you say—meaning only that they were down 5 percent, hardly an earth-shaking crisis. But by the time those words get passed around through five or six people in the rumor chain, they turn into, "It looks like we're going into Chapter 11 soon." Watch what you say—you can have a huge impact without meaning to.

Work on the next exercise to pinpoint your particular contribution.

# Exercise:
## *My Contributions to the Nightmare*

1. What possible contributions am I making to the problem?

_____

_____

_____

_____

_____

2. What steps could I take to gain more influence over the situation?

_____

_____

_____

_____

_____

3. What emotions am I experiencing because of the situation, and how might they be affecting the others involved?

_____

_____

_____

_____

_____

## Face the Problem Head On (Communicate!)

You can't stamp out the rumor mill, nor should you try. You can only take a balanced and professional approach to it, understanding that helping to manage this "grapevine" is part of your job.

If you discover specific malicious people who use office gossip to hurt others and the "word to the wise" approach isn't effective with them, prepare for a no-nonsense dialogue with them by using the following worksheet.

# Exercise:
## *Giving Negative Feedback Worksheet*

1. Define the problem in behavioral terms.

_____

_____

_____

_____

2. Relate the impact and your feelings.

_____

_____

_____

_____

Ask—then *listen!*—for the real problem.

_____

_____

_____

_____

1. Work out a win/win change.

_____

_____

_____

2. Focus on the positive elements of the relationship.

_____

_____

_____

## Make a Plan

Employees use gossip and backbiting for a variety of reasons, from professional jealousy to personality conflict to misplaced affection. You need to focus on redirecting the situation back to the work itself. In extreme cases, reassignment or separation may be necessary.

Let's return to the various "faces" of the rumor mill to consider the best strategy:

**Job-related rumors.** The right attitude here is to act as if the employee is offering you job-related information or asking a job-related question. Listen attentively and calmly to what the person has to say ("I heard that a new round of layoffs is due next month!"), and then treat it as a job inquiry. ("Please tell me what you've been told"). When the employee finishes, say, "Thanks for bringing this to me. Let me look into it." Then investigate the situation. Depending on what you find, use your discretion and good judgment in getting back to the employee (you can't, of course, share confidential information).

**Personal gossip.** If it's not a job-related rumor ("I heard that Sally and John had a hot date Saturday night!"), act in a noncommittal fashion. "That's interesting," you can say in a normal voice. Don't ask questions, inquire, or criticize the person for telling you. You need to give the impression of not having a feeling one way or another. You'll end up getting much less of that sort of gossip, which is exactly what you want, while not closing the door to other information that might be valuable.

**Hostile rumors.** You normally have a hard time catching someone in the act of spreading a nasty tidbit, but fortunately it's not necessary to do so. Talk to your suspect in private, and without being accusatory, say that you're aware someone is spreading a malicious rumor and that you won't tolerate that sort of behavior. Ask if he or she knows anything about it. Your suspect will almost certainly deny it. Instead of arguing or accusing, just ask to be informed if he or she hears anything. Notice that you've made it clear you won't stand for the behavior as well as whom you suspect. In most cases, you'll discover that the rumor mongering stops.

## Decide What to Do If Dialogue Doesn't Work

If you have an employee spreading malicious rumors, and the earlier strategies haven't worked, you have to take further action. You'll need some behavioral evidence first, and it's hard to catch the person in the act. Instead, you can approach it from the perspective that you keep hearing that Employee X is spreading malicious rumors. Employee X denies it. You reply that you have no reason to doubt Employee X, but you don't want to hear the rumor that Employee X is doing this. Both you and the employee know what's going on, but you haven't stepped over the line of making accusations you can't prove.

If the behavior still doesn't stop, you can use the circumstantial evidence you've collected as a way to take action, from counseling on into the formal disciplinary process.

# Help! [Your Nightmare Here]: A Do-It-Yourself Model

Your nightmare may or may not resemble the situations in this book. As Sigmund Freud said, "Every happy family is alike. Every unhappy family is miserable in its own unique way." Although there's a rich variety of supervisory nightmares, to deal with yours you need only apply the model approach presented throughout this book. By now, you've seen the multistep process in operation and can apply it to your own situation. This chapter reviews the five-step model and provides worksheets you can use to work through your personal nightmare.

## 1. Diagnose the situation in behavioral terms.

- Use the Incident Log to measure the problem over a two-week period, and then the Behavioral Language exercise to describe it properly (write down the nightmare in your own words, and then go through the description looking for judgmental language and change it to a behavioral description).

## 2. Recognize and deal with your contributions.

- Define what steps you could take to gain more influence over the situation.

- Define what emotions you're experiencing because of the situation, and how they might be affecting the others involved.

- If appropriate, list the jobs the affected person does differently and better than you.

### 3. Face the problem head on (communicate!).

- Refer to your behavioral description of the problem.

- Write out how you plan to approach each element of G-R-E-A-T (Goals, Roles, Expectations, Abilities, and Time).

- If you need to offer negative feedback:

  - Define the problem in behavioral terms.

  - Relate the impact and your feelings.

  - Ask—then *listen!*—for the real problem.

  - Work out a win/win change.

  - Focus on the positive elements of the relationship.

### 4. Make a plan.

- Document the steps you will take as well as those you need the other person to be responsible for.

- If the plan involves empowering independent work, answer the following questions:

  - Which parts of the work can be performed independently?

  - Which parts of the work can't be performed independently?

  - Is the employee able to perform these tasks in a satisfactory manner without supervision?

  - If not, can training, tools, or job redesign make him or her better able to work independently?

### 5. Decide what to do if dialogue doesn't work.

- Review the results of the previous dialogues.
- Review the seriousness of the issue.
- Make it clear what you expect.
- Provide clear and consistent supervision.
- Work on the interpersonal issues.
- Have a formal development conference.
- Take formal disciplinary action.

***Good luck!***

# Incident Log Format

I perceive the following behavior(s) in employee _____ :

| When | What | Impact |
|------|------|--------|
|      |      |        |
|      |      |        |
|      |      |        |
|      |      |        |
|      |      |        |

Actual incidence of the behavior(s) over a two-week period:

| Day | Incident Log |
|-----|--------------|
| Day 1 | |
| Day 2 | |
| Day 3 | |
| Day 4 | |
| Day 5 | |
| Day 6 | |
| Day 7 | |
| Day 8 | |
| Day 9 | |
| Day 10 | |

My perception was:  ☐ Confirmed        ☐ Not confirmed
                          by the Incident Log          by the Incident Log

# Behavioral Language

Write down a supervisory nightmare you are currently experiencing.

_____

_____

_____

_____

_____

_____

_____

_____

_____

_____

Now go through your written description looking for judgmental language (language that presupposes you know reasons or motives) and change it to descriptive language (language describing what you observe behaviorally that suggests there is a problem). Be as specific as you can.

1. Judgmental Language _____

   Behavior You Actually Observe _____

2. Judgmental Language _____

   Behavior You Actually Observe _____

3. Judgmental Language _____

   Behavior You Actually Observe _____

4. Judgmental Language _____

   Behavior You Actually Observe _____

5. Judgmental Language _____

   Behavior You Actually Observe _____

# My Contributions to the Nightmare

1. What steps could I take to gain more influence over the situation?

_____

_____

_____

_____

_____

_____

2. What emotions am I experiencing because of the situation, and how might they be affecting the other people involved?

_____

_____

_____

_____

_____

_____

_____

# Competency Issues

List the jobs the affected person does differently and better than you.

_____

_____

_____

_____

_____

# Prepare to Have GREAT Communication

**Step 1:** Write a behavioral description of the problem.

_____

_____

_____

_____

_____

_____

_____

_____

**Step 2:** Decide how you plan to approach each element of G-R-E-A-T.

- **Goals:** What is the behavioral goal or goals you would like to achieve? How would things be different if you got the change you wanted? What are the reasons you want or need to achieve these goals?

_____

_____

_____

_____

_____

_____

_____

- **Roles:** What are the roles you want to play and have the other person play in your work situation? (Check that they are defined in behavioral terms.)

My Role                                Their Role

_____                _____

_____                _____

_____                _____

_____                _____

_____                _____

_____                _____

- **Expectations:** What are your expectations for satisfactory performance? For outstanding performance? Have expectations changed from previous situations? How do you expect to be treated? How do you expect a good employee to act when there is a problem?

_____

_____

_____

_____

_____

- **Abilities:** Is the problem a "Don't Know, "Can't Do," or "Won't Do"? (Always assume it's a "Don't Know" first, then escalate—you'll be more successful that way.)

☐ **Don't Know:** How can I best give the information or instruction in behavioral terms?

_____

_____

_____

_____

_____

☐ **Can't Do:** Could the employee do the job for $10 million?

☐ Yes   ☐ No

If not, it's a "can't do" problem. What steps could you take to help the employee become able to do the job?

- Training: _____

- Changes in the job structure: _____

_____

- Tools and resources: _____

_____

- Reassignment: _____

_____

☐ **Won't Do:** What are the rewards and punishments (from the team member's point of view) for refusing to do the job the way it needs to be done?

- Performance is punished (list negative consequences of doing the job correctly):

_____

_____

_____

_____

_____

- Failure is rewarded (list positive consequences of not doing the job correctly):

_____

_____

_____

_____

_____

• Performance doesn't matter (why not?):

_____

_____

_____

_____

List ways you can change the rewards and punishments to achieve the desired behavioral change.

• **Time:** What is your timetable? Is this an "instantaneous change" situation or one calling for gradual, steady improvement? What support will you provide? How will you measure progress toward the goal?

_____

_____

_____

_____

_____

## The Negative Feedback Model

**Step 1:** Describe the problem with the know-it-all employee in behavioral terms. (If necessary, first write it in emotional and judgmental language, then edit it.)

_____

_____

_____

_____

_____

_____

**Step 2:** Tell the person about your concerns, using the Negative Feedback Model.

1. Define the problem in behavioral terms (use a specific incident or two; don't be general).

   _____

   _____

   _____

   _____

2. Relate the impact and your feelings (how it affected you or others; how it affected the work to be done).

   _____

   _____

   _____

   _____

3. Ask—then *listen!*—for the real problem (what did you hope to achieve? how could we change?).

   _____

   _____

   _____

   _____

   _____

4. Work out a win/win change (what will you both do?).

   _____

   _____

   _____

   _____

   _____

5. Focus on the positive elements of the relationship (his or her desire to contribute, the good ideas presented).

_____

_____

_____

_____

_____

_____

## Action Plan Worksheet

What I Will Do/By When          What You Will Do/By When

_____          _____

_____          _____

_____          _____

_____          _____

## Empowering Independent Work

1. Which parts of the work can be performed independently?

_____

_____

_____

_____

2. Which parts of the work cannot be performed independently?

_____

_____

_____

_____

3. Is the employee able to perform these tasks in a satisfactory manner without supervision?

_____

_____

_____

_____

4. If not, can training, tools, or job redesign make the employee better able to work independently?

_____

_____

_____

_____

5. Decide what to do if dialogue doesn't work.

_____

_____

_____

_____

## Next Step Options Worksheet

Review the results of the previous dialogues.

_____

_____

_____

Review the seriousness of the issue.

_____

_____

_____

Make it clear what you expect.

_____

_____

_____

_____

Provide clear and consistent supervision.

_____

_____

_____

_____

Work on the interpersonal issues.

_____

_____

_____

_____

Have a formal development conference.

_____

_____

_____

_____

Take formal disciplinary action.

_____

_____

_____

_____

# Bibliography
# and Suggested
# Reading

Dana, Daniel. *Talk It Out! Four Steps to Managing People Problems in Your Organization.* Amherst, MA: Human Resources Development Press, 1989.

Eigen, Barry. *How to Think Like a Boss: And Get Ahead at Work.* New York: Carol Publishing Group, 1990.

Fuller, George. *The First-Time Supervisor's Survival Guide.* Englewood Cliffs, NJ: Prentice Hall, 1995.

Gagnon, Gene. *Supervising on the Line: A Self-Help Guide for First-Line Supervisors.* Minnetonka, MN: Margo, 1988.

Keirsey, David, and Marilyn Bates. *Please Understand Me: Character and Temperament Types.* Del Mar, CA: Prometheus Nemesis Book Company, 1984.

Loen, Raymond. *Superior Supervision: The 10% Solution.* New York: Lexington Books, 1994.

McGraw, Robert. *Learning to Laugh at Work.* Mission, KS: SkillPath Publications, 1995.

Wylie, Peter. *Problem Employees: How to Improve Their Performance.* Dover, NH: Upstart Publications, 1991.

# Available From SkillPath Publications

## Self-Study Sourcebooks

*Climbing the Corporate Ladder: What You Need to Know and Do to Be a Promotable Person*
  by Barbara Pachter and Marjorie Brody

*Coping With Supervisory Nightmares: 12 Common Nightmares of Leadership and What You
  Can Do About Them* by Michael and Deborah Singer Dobson

*Defeating Procrastination: 52 Fail-Safe Tips for Keeping Time on Your Side*
  by Marlene Caroselli, Ed.D.

*Discovering Your Purpose* by Ivy Haley

*Going for the Gold: Winning the Gold Medal for Financial Independence* by Lesley D. Bissett, CFP

*Having Something to Say When You Have to Say Something: The Art of Organizing Your
  Presentation* by Randy Horn

*Info-Flood: How to Swim in a Sea of Information Without Going Under* by Marlene Caroselli, Ed.D.

*The Innovative Secretary* by Marlene Caroselli, Ed.D.

*Letters & Memos: Just Like That!* by Dave Davies

*Mastering the Art of Communication: Your Keys to Developing a More Effective Personal Style*
  by Michelle Fairfield Poley

*Organized for Success! 95 Tips for Taking Control of Your Time, Your Space, and Your Life*
  by Nanci McGraw

*A Passion to Lead! How to Develop Your Natural Leadership Ability* by Michael Plumstead

*P.E.R.S.U.A.D.E.: Communication Strategies That Move People to Action*
  by Marlene Caroselli, Ed.D.

*Productivity Power: 250 Great Ideas for Being More Productive* by Jim Temme

*Promoting Yourself: 50 Ways to Increase Your Prestige, Power, and Paycheck*
  by Marlene Caroselli, Ed.D.

*Risk-Taking: 50 Ways to Turn Risks Into Rewards* by Marlene Caroselli, Ed.D. and David Harris

*Speak Up and Stand Out: How to Make Effective Presentations* by Nanci McGraw

*Stress Control: How You Can Find Relief From Life's Daily Stress* by Steve Bell

*The Technical Writer's Guide* by Robert McGraw

*Total Quality Customer Service: How to Make It Your Way of Life* by Jim Temme

*Write It Right! A Guide for Clear and Correct Writing* by Richard Andersen and Helene Hinis

*Your Total Communication Image* by Janet Signe Olson, Ph.D.

## Handbooks

*The ABC's of Empowered Teams: Building Blocks for Success* by Mark Towers

*Assert Yourself! Developing Power-Packed Communication Skills to Make Your Points Clearly,
  Confidently, and Persuasively* by Lisa Contini

*Breaking the Ice: How to Improve Your On-the-Spot Communication Skills* by Deborah Shouse

*The Care and Keeping of Customers: A Treasury of Facts, Tips and Proven Techniques for Keeping Your Customers Coming BACK!* by Roy Lantz

*Challenging Change: Five Steps for Dealing With Change* by Holly DeForest and Mary Steinberg

*Dynamic Delegation: A Manager's Guide for Active Empowerment* by Mark Towers

*Every Woman's Guide to Career Success* by Denise M. Dudley

*Hiring and Firing: What Every Manager Needs to Know* by Marlene Caroselli, Ed.D. with Laura Wyeth, Ms.Ed.

*How to Be a More Effective Group Communicator: How to Find Your Role and Boost Your Confidence in Group Situations* by Deborah Shouse

*How to Deal With Difficult People* by Paul Friedman

*Learning to Laugh at Work: The Power of Humor in the Workplace* by Robert McGraw

*Making Your Mark: How to Develop a Personal Marketing Plan for Becoming More Visible and More Appreciated at Work* by Deborah Shouse

*Meetings That Work* by Marlene Caroselli, Ed.D.

*The Mentoring Advantage: How to Help Your Career Soar to New Heights* by Pam Grout

*Minding Your Business Manners: Etiquette Tips for Presenting Yourself Professionally in Every Business Situation* by Marjorie Brody and Barbara Pachter

*Misspeller's Guide* by Joel and Ruth Schroeder

*Motivation in the Workplace: How to Motivate Workers to Peak Performance and Productivity* by Barbara Fielder

*NameTags Plus: Games You Can Play When People Don't Know What to Say* by Deborah Shouse

*Networking: How to Creatively Tap Your People Resources* by Colleen Clarke

*New & Improved! 25 Ways to Be More Creative and More Effective* by Pam Grout

*The Power of Positivity: Eighty Ways to Energize Your Life* by Joel and Ruth Schroeder

*Power Write! A Practical Guide to Words That Work* by Helene Hinis

*Putting Anger to Work For You!* by Ruth and Joel Schroeder

*Reinventing Your Self: 28 Strategies for Coping With Change* by Mark Towers

*Saying "No" to Negativity: How to Manage Negativity in Yourself, Your Boss and Your Co-Workers* by Zoie Kaye

*The Supervisor's Guide: The Everyday Guide to Coordinating People and Tasks* by Jerry Brown and Denise Dudley, Ph.D.

*Taking Charge: A Personal Guide to Managing Projects and Priorities* by Michal E. Feder

*Treasure Hunt: 10 Stepping Stones to a New and More Confident You!* by Pam Grout

*A Winning Attitude: How to Develop Your Most Important Asset!* by Michelle Fairfield Poley

**For more information, call 1-800-873-7545.**

# Notes

# Notes